EDITOR'S NOTE

WHEN WE LAUNCHED OUR BRIEFS SERIES in 2016, we knew the books would be a hit: briefer (of course) even than our already-concise standard titles, and therefore a deeper dive within a tighter scope, like a shot of espresso rather than a cup of coffee. And the twelve titles that emerged certainly delivered, offering readers quick learning on specific topics within web design, development, and content.

What we didn't expect was how much readers would request these titles in print. We intended for the Briefs series to be digital-only—and in 2016, that sounded like a solid bet. All around us, publishers were singing the praises of ebooks and claiming that paper was an artifact of the past. But even—or perhaps especially—within our audience of tech workers, readers asked for tangible reading experiences.

We closed the Briefs series after twelve amazing titles, but they continue to teach readers new skills, and deserve their own moment of ink. So we've brought them together in three new anthologies, available in a special edition printed hardcover format.

Volume 2, the Design and Content Anthology, covers practitioner fundamentals like pricing and presenting design work, and creating and sustaining writing and content practices. We hope this collection of Briefs continues to reach readers in a meaningful way.

2

A BOOK APART

PRICING DESIGN

DAN MALL

FOREWORD BY
MIKE MONTEIRO

BRIEFS

Publisher: Jeffrey Zeldman
Designer: Jason Santa Maria
Executive Director: Katel LeDû
Editor: Tina Lee
Technical Editor: Jason Blumer
Copyeditor: Lisa Maria Martin
Proofreader: Caren Litherland
Compositor: Rob Weychert
Ebook Producer: Ron Bilodeau

ISBN: 978-1-9375573-7-9

A Book Apart
New York, New York
http://abookapart.com

10 9 8 7 6 5 4 3 2 1

TABLE OF CONTENTS: PRICING DESIGN

FOREWORD

YOU ARE GOING TO make more money from this book than you spent on it.

You are going to read it—probably more than once. You're going to highlight quite a few passages. You're going to have your fair share of "aha" moments. You're going to take the lessons to heart. And eventually, you're going to make adjustments to how you price your work based on what you'll read here. You'll be more confident. You'll ask for more than you've asked for before. And if you're good at what you do, you'll get it. You'll start making more money for yourself. Your business will grow. And you may even hire some people to help you with the newfound work.

You are going to make more money from this book than Dan Mall ever will.

Dan is okay with that. Because that's what Dan does for a living. He builds value. And as a designer, Dan understands that his clients will make more money from his work than he ever will, especially if he does it right. And quite honestly, that's the key to pricing work. Understanding that the people you're doing it for stand to benefit considerably if you do it right. And that's why Dan charges them according to the value of the work. Because Dan makes money for people.

And yet, designers (and I love you all) get so weird about money. We hem and haw when it comes up. Our hands get clammy. Our hearts start racing. We start sweating. We hope the client brings it up so we don't have to. Money makes us nervous. And there's absolutely no reason for this. Everyone who will ever hire you has exchanged money for services. They probably exchanged money for coffee this very morning. It's a daily occurrence. So treat it that way.

Dan gets it. And like all of us, he learned some of those lessons the hard way. And because he's a good guy, he wants to share what he's learned with you. Because he wants you to be happy, pay your bills, and have a good career.

You should listen to him.

—Mike Monteiro

INTRODUCTION

I WANT TO help you make more money.

Maybe this story sounds familiar. When I went out on my own, after a decade at more than a few agencies, I settled on charging $100/hour, as that's what I'd heard most freelancers charged. Clients hardly pushed back. Projects went well, and I raised my rates—I got to $150/hour before customers balked. Agencies would contact me to do design comps for $150/hour, up to $1,500. (I eventually learned this was shorthand for "We think this shouldn't take more than ten hours." More on this later.) By then, I could do a round of work in about three hours, which meant 1) I'd make $450, and 2) I'd leave a lot of money on the table.

So I tried an experiment. On the next project, when I asked, "How much do you want to spend?" and they said, "One hundred and fifty dollars per hour, up to fifteen hundred," I countered with a flat fee of $1,000. I was happy because it was way more than $450 (I was always pretty good at estimating my hours), and my client was happy because it was still less than their budget: win-win.

It worked so well, I was soon booking five months out, and that's when I met Esther—and doubled down on this whole pricing enterprise.

Esther (not her real name) came through a friend's referral. She was an entrepreneur, with a great idea for a site she wanted to build from scratch. When we talked about her project, I reckoned it'd be a six-month effort. Given my existing work pipeline, I'd be booked for most of the year, and I didn't want to be that locked down. Worse, what if I agreed to the project, turning down others, only to have Esther bail just before we got rolling?

So I gave her the "go away" price. You know the one. You quote some ridiculously high number that the client wouldn't possibly pay. To sidestep the slight chance that she *would,* I added extra repellent. (I know I could've politely declined, but I hadn't yet developed the muscle of saying no to good projects.)

I emailed Esther a "Save the Date" contract:

You agree to pay a one-time, additional, nonrefundable fee of $7,000. This ensures that the October date will be held for your project.

Esther never responded.

Five days later, I received a check for $7,000 in the mail.

I learned a terrific lesson that day: people will pay for things they value, no matter how wildly out of reach you might think it is.

This is a book about making more money—about knowing your worth, your value. It's a book about understanding what your clients want, and doing the best work you can for them.

Pricing feels fraught, but it isn't once you put some definition around it and put it into practice a few times. It's a crucial part of business, so set your mind on getting better about it. I'm here to help you figure out what price to name—the one that simultaneously makes you rich and sounds like a steal for your clients. I'll share examples of pricing gone wrong and pricing gone so, so right.

This book is for you.

1

PRICING METHODS

WE'RE LUCKY. Our profession pays well, because we've convinced our clients that design is important (and it is). But few of us price properly to capitalize on that importance. Almost every freelancer and agency owner I talk to says the same thing when I ask why they price the way they do: "It's all I know, because that's how they did it at my last company."

For as much as we question and reinvent our processes and project deliverables, few of us take the time to question—to *design*—how we price. We tend to assume there's only one method, whether it's an old way or something a friend tipped us on.

In reality, we can price projects in many ways. Let's inventory the most common and assess each of their benefits and drawbacks:

1. Industry standard
2. Cost-plus
3. Opportunity cost

(Heads up: this book does contain some math. Should you become nauseated or light-headed, math-sick bags are located on the back of the seat in front of you. And don't worry, we all start out this way. The more you practice pricing, the easier the math part gets.)

INDUSTRY STANDARD

This is also known as a *market rate*. As the word *standard* suggests, this means your rate lines up more or less with everyone else's.

The easiest way to come up with an industry-standard rate is to survey your friends' rates. Say you chat with your designer pal Lindsay, who says she charges $125/hour. Then you ask Michael, who charges $90/hour. You also ask Tobias, who charges $80/hour. You average those rates to land at $98.33/hour, and you round up to $100/hour because the math is easier. Presto: your market rate.

So far, so good. The problem is that market rates tend to work against you, unless you're at the bottom of the pile—that industry standard just telegraphs, "Well, I'm not worse than anyone else." Let's say a prospective client is deciding among you and your three friends. If all of you have roughly the same level of experience and similar-caliber portfolios, who do you think the client will choose?

Most likely, it's the person with the lowest rate: in this case, Tobias, at $80/hour. This pricing strategy—setting cheaper rates than your competitors and hoping you get more work to accommodate the price drop—is called *penetration pricing*. It's difficult to bank on (get it?), and most economists suggest using it sparingly and only for a limited time. If you're Tobias, you'll win work, but you won't do yourself any favors in the long run.

I'm coming down hard on market rates, but I believe they're only a good place to start if you don't know yet what to do. (Hey, I started that way too.) They don't scale as you gain more experience. The minute you become better and more desirable than your peers and competitors, you've outgrown industry standard pricing.

COST-PLUS

With cost-plus, you calculate your costs—overhead, salaries, miscellaneous expenses—and add some percentage on top of that to ensure profit. Your costs can be expressed hourly, weekly, monthly, or for any time period; the logic still applies.

When I started freelancing, I tallied all my bills for the month to see how much I cost (**FIG 1.1**).

At the minimum, if I made $7,038.95/month, I would break even. So I added a little padding, or *margin*—42% to be exact—to make sure I'd always turn a profit. I set a goal to make $10,000/month, which would give me an extra $2,961.05 to save for a rainy day. This is cost-plus: $7,038.95 was the cost, $2,961.05 was the *plus,* and $10,000 was the monthly rate I quoted to anyone who inquired (**FIG 1.2**).

The main driver for using cost-plus is its simplicity: calculate your break-even number, add a little on top (most agencies go

FIG 1.1: A roundup of my monthly bills.

ITEM	COST
Health insurance	$472.62
Gym	$79.98
Mortgage	$700
TV services	$25.99
Auto expenses	$887.27
Groceries	$400
Misc. shopping	$407
Student loan	$128.09
Taxes	$1000
Phone	$200
Water	$80
Electric	$125.00
Tithe	$400
Property tax	$100
Sewer dept.	$33
Miscellaneous	$2,000
Total	**$7,038.95**

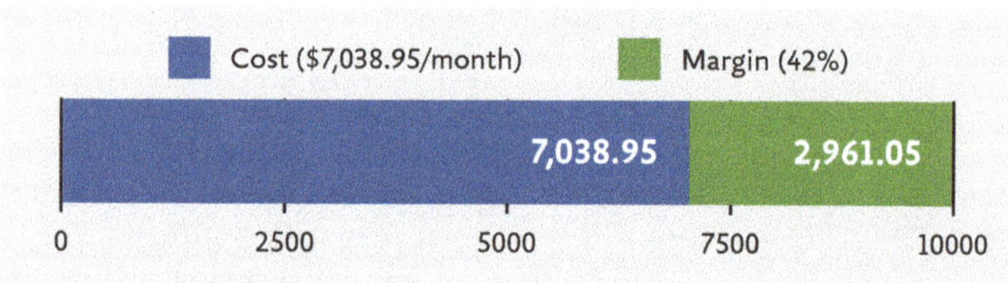

FIG 1.2: Cost-plus visualized: cost + margin = price.

for somewhere between a 15% and 50% margin), and you have your rate. My CPA likes to say that even his eight-year-old knows to charge more for her lemonade than the total cost of supplies.

But cost-plus has a big drawback—it's all about one thing: you. Pricing is like the tango; it takes two. Using cost-plus to land on a rate completely independent of your customer has a great deal of inflexibility. Because I calculated *my* costs and built in *my* desired margin long before any client showed up, I don't have much space to work with clients who can't afford my rate, unless I trim my margins or eat into my costs—both undesirable. I also can't benefit from clients who are willing and able to pay well over my rate because they believe they're getting way more in return.

We work in a service business; a pricing approach that doesn't honor half of the relationship is, by definition, lopsided.

OPPORTUNITY COST

The last route to a rate is tough to quantify, but it considers your priorities, what your client wants, what you bring to the table, and what you're willing to pass up.

My friend Robert is always up for a dare; all our friends know this. Whenever we get together, we often find ourselves offering him $20 to eat a ghost pepper or $50 to spill his beverage on the adjacent table or $100 to knock over that kid's ice cream cone.

Though it's hard to say what goes through Robert's head—seriously, why is he even friends with us?—I'd imagine he weighs the cost of his actions and any sacrifice against the return. Setting his mouth on fire for a few minutes is worth $20; making a kid sad is not worth any amount. (Robert's such a sweetheart.)

That's what a rate based on opportunity cost is about: Is the gain worth the price?

Consider this scenario. For one hour of work, you'll receive a nice crisp C-note (**FIG 1.3**).

FIG 1.3: An opportunity-cost approach asks what you're willing to give up and what you'd want in return.

In return, you'll give up:

- an hour of playing your new video game
- an hour of playing with your kids
- an hour of feeling the burn at the gym
- an hour of picking up crochet as a hobby

You get the idea. Is that hour a fair trade to you? If so, $100/hour fits the bill. If you'd rather spend that hour getting chiseled calves, then $100/hour is too low; you'll likely need to increase that rate.

But wait—how do clients fit into this? While you're weighing your proposed trade, your client is considering the same question: Is what I'm getting better than what I'm giving up?

The cool part about this type of pricing is that it puts you and your client on even footing. But it's also the method that people are least comfortable with, because it can't be derived from a formula. (If only there were a way to back your gut with sound, persuasive examples of what's worthwhile to the client... we'll get to that.)

Your job as a professional is to create things for your clients that boost their business, and price them in a way that both works out on a spreadsheet and (more important) feels good in the gut—for both of you.

"WHAT'S YOUR RATE?"

Now that we've covered the three general rationales for pricing, you can describe the outcome of that pricing to your customers as a *time-based rate* or a *fixed price*.

Time-based rates

The common advice you'll hear when starting out is to charge hourly, mostly because it's what everyone else does. (Industry standard, remember?) This often comes from reputable sources. AIGA has some tips on calculating a freelance rate (http://bkaprt.com/pd/01-01/), as does Treehouse (http://bkaprt.com/pd/01-02/). HOW lays out average hourly rates across the US to help you see if your rate is on par with everyone else's (http://bkaprt.com/pd/01-03/).

From my experience, freelance designers and developers charge anywhere from $50/hour on the low end to $150/hour on the high end. Agencies typically charge a bit more, partly because they have higher overhead, but mostly because they can. Some agencies have a *rate card,* shared with clients, that lists an hourly rate for each role (**FIG 1.4**).

Other agencies opt for a simpler *blended hourly rate,* which can be calculated in a couple ways. You can:

1. **Average your rates.** In our example, one hour of this agency's time for all team members costs $1,300. Divide that by eight team members, and the blended rate is $162.50/hour. It's lower than the principal rate, but a bit higher than the junior rate; the agency makes more money off the blended rate if the juniors bill more hours than the seniors.
2. **Use past experience.** Look at a prior project that's similar in scope. Say that project took 360 hours and you charged $67,000. Some quick math ($67,000 / 360 hours) gives you a blended rate of $186.11/hour, which you can now charge your new customer.

Hourly pricing is easy to grasp—the more you work, the more you get paid. If you're comfortable with that, you can

FIG 1.4: A sample rate card for agency roles.

ROLE	RATE
Principal	$250/hour
Creative Director	$200/hour
Technology Director	$200/hour
Senior Designer	$150/hour
Senior Developer	$150/hour
Senior Copywriter	$150/hour
Junior Designer	$100/hour
Junior Developer	$100/hour

put this book down and go forth to charge. Thanks for reading, and best of luck to you. We'll even send you a prorated refund for the pages you didn't read, and we'll subsequently go out of business. (Foreshadowing!)

Beyond hourly rates (the most common), other variations include daily, weekly, or monthly rates. They each have pros and cons, but they all suffer from the same major setback: directly tying your revenue to your effort. Let's look at how this breaks down.

People want prices up front

A brand-new restaurant opens in your town, and you nab a reservation for its first night. You open the menu and none of the items has a price next to it, so you order your favorites: an heirloom tomato salad, the surf and turf, a side of seasonal vegetables, a bottle of wine, and a cheesecake to top it all off. It's one of the most delicious meals you've ever had.

And then you get the bill.

It's *hundreds* of dollars more than you expected to pay. Suddenly, you second-guess your choices. Perhaps you could have had an eight-ounce steak instead of the surf and turf. Perhaps the seasonal vegetables were overkill after the salad. You didn't really drink *that* much wine, so maybe you should have gotten a glass instead. And did you really need that dessert?

But it's too late, because you've already eaten the meal. You can't regurgitate and return it, even though you now wish you could. This is what your customers go through when you bill them hourly. People like knowing the price of an item or service *before* they commit to purchasing it—it's how we assess what's worth paying. Think of everything you might have paid for in the last week: groceries, clothes, dry cleaning, new equipment, books. All of these things have a price up front, and you can decide for yourself whether they're worth parting with your hard-earned money.

An ever-changing bill does no one favors. Really. It doesn't help your costs when you come in way under hours, and you're scrambling to make up the difference at month's end. And a project worth $10,000 to the client might not be worth $12,000, but they won't find that out until you've done the work and sent the bill. The best transactions—and ones that stand a chance of repeating!—are beneficial for the seller *and* the buyer.

Value is relative

If I walk up to you and say, "Here's a candy bar. That'll be $100," your brain would immediately whir to assess what makes that candy bar worth $100. The first step is to compare it with every other candy bar you've had in your life. Recalling that you've paid roughly $1 for most of them, you then hypothesize why this particular bar's value is significantly more. Maybe its ingredients include some rare form of chocolate, imported from a remote part of the world few have access to. Maybe it grants you special powers, like temporary X-ray vision or the ability to extinguish student loans. And if you conclude that this candy bar is pretty similar to others you've eaten, you probably won't leap to spend an extra $99.

If I instead approach someone who hasn't ever heard of a candy bar before, they have a far more difficult decision because they can't rely on past experience. So the candy bar gets compared to other things that cost $100. Is it worth as much as that necklace? That jacket? This lamp?

When you tell a client that you have an hourly rate, they compare you with all the other people they know to have hourly rates. They might think:

- Fast-food workers make minimum wage. High school students, or younger people, tend to work those jobs.
- Plumbers, electricians, or professionals in similar trades make more. Most have gone to school and obtained a license. (Unless they're a friend's "I know a person," who comes dirt cheap and learned by watching YouTube videos.)
- Lawyers and doctors cost an arm and a leg. But their level of training is intense—spanning a decade or more for doctors—and they've conquered rigorous exams. They also deal with the most sensitive information, and, in some cases, literally save lives.

This is the frame of reference you go up against when you say you bill by the hour. When I started freelancing, I found it incredibly difficult to get more than $150/hour, because my customers slotted my skills alongside those of their plumber or electrician. Perhaps they thought what I did was a one-time service like unclogging the drain, or maybe they had a niece that took a class in high school on building websites, and they couldn't tell the difference between what she could do and what I could do. No matter the reason, framing sales through hourly rates makes this type of comparison easy for a client.

Hourly rates don't grow as you do

Think back to when you started designing. You graduated high school and stumbled on a completely legal copy of Photoshop. Remember your first customer? That friend of a friend who needed a flyer for her real estate business? You charged her $50/hour, because you heard that was the going rate. She agreed; you were proud. It took you ten hours, and you made $500. You were living the dream.

Fast-forward to now. You have five years of experience under your belt. You've worked at a few agencies, and you're in a pretty senior position. But that doesn't stop Ms. Real Estate from coming back. She trusts you, and she needs a new flyer. You oblige. You've doubled your rate, as $100/hour is closer to the industry standard. She agrees; you're still proud. With all that experience you have, you finish the flyer in five hours, half the time it took you half a decade ago. You make $500. You're living the drea—wait a sec. You made the same amount of money that you made way back then? How does that make sense? Why are you being penalized for your experience and efficiency?

Let's redo the scenario. To turn a better profit, you quadruple your rate to $200/hour. But this time, Ms. Real Estate refuses, because she can't stomach paying four times as much as the last time. Sad trombone.

Even worse: while your customer stared down the barrel of a quadruple increase ($50/hour → $200/hour), you only would have made twice as much ($500 → $1000). It's a lose-lose situation.

Misaligned incentives

With hourly billing, the more time you spend on the project, the more money you gain. However, the more time you spend, the more money your customer loses. This is when customers ask, "Shouldn't that only take an hour instead of four?" Not necessarily because they think it should, but because they want it to! From the outset, you and the customer are in conflict, because your incentives are on opposite ends of the spectrum.

Setting a time-based rate shines a spotlight on the fact that more work equals less money in your client's bank account. But you want them to focus on all the benefits your work will bring them, not what they'll give up.

Artificial ceilings

If you're billing your time, you've placed an artificial ceiling on the amount you can make. Say you have forty billable hours in a week and fifty-two weeks in a year, which works out to 2,080 billable hours in one year—if you don't take vacation or get sick. Assuming a rate of $100/hour, you make an annual $208,000 if you are 100% billable. While that's not a small chunk of dough, it's an arbitrary limit.

Let's take an extreme example. You've decided to work *every* hour of the year. (You go, Captain Ambitious.) One (non-leap) year holds 8,760 hours. At $100/hour, you can make $876,000 if you are 100% billable. Again, it's a lot of money, but how are people out there making millions?

Because we all have the same amount of time, it's not a differentiator for anyone. And since you can't create more time, the only thing to do is increase your hourly rate. But you've seen how difficult it is to convince customers to pay over a certain rate. The combined limitations of time and rates make for ineffective variables in raising your income.

Fixed prices

Fixed prices are slightly more beneficial for your customers because they offer something that time-based rates don't: judgment. Customers can look at a fixed price, compare it to what they're getting, and determine whether it's worth the money *before* you both agree to do the project together.

Fixed prices appeal because they appear to solve the plight of experienced designers who zip to a project's finish. Unfortunately, the methodology to derive a fixed price is often based on an hourly price, a line of reasoning that sinks you from the start. You might've gone through this scenario:

***Client:** I want a website.*
***You:** That'll be $10,000.*
***Client:** What's that based on?*
***You:** Um...[struggles to come up with a reason on the spot] I think it'll take about 100 hours and I usually charge $100/hour.*

Annnnnnnnd welcome back to all the downsides of time-based rates. Even worse, you don't have a rationale that holds water if you want to increase your price—without increasing your time on the project.

I've seen people try to beat this system two ways. Some designers give in to temptation and pad their hourly estimate

ROLE	RATE
Director Client Services	$533/hour
Executive Director Account Planning	$601/hour
Executive Research Director	$427/hour
Chief Creative Director	$964/hour
Executive Media Director	$478/hour
Executive Director Print Production	$391/hour

FIG 1.5: These astronomical numbers emphasize just how unsustainable it is to raise hourly rates.

to land on a bigger fixed price. I have a word for that: *lying*. It starts innocently enough; they're trying to find a way around the constraint that time is finite. But make no mistake: this is unethical. Your pricing methodology is the foundation of how you do business. If your foundation is rotten, the fruits that grow from it will be rotten too.

Others work the other end of the equation and hike up their hourly rates. Remember the agency rate card we saw earlier? Advertising Age reported on a survey taken in 2008 on the average billing rates of New York ad agencies with over 500 employees (http://bkaprt.com/pd/01-04/). It's clear that, to make a project worth their while and talents, these agencies have to lean on pretty ridiculous figures (**FIG 1.5**).

You can see right through these rates. $964/hour? Come on! If you think persuading a client to spend more than $150/hour—as I have—was difficult, imagine trying to talk them into three times what they pay their lawyer.

Pocket knives and atom bombs

A last thought: a common defense of charging for time—whether as an hourly rate or the basis for a fixed price—is that it gives you the ability to allow for shifting requirements or clients who can't seem to make up their minds about what they want. In other words, most professionals who charge for time use pricing to solve a scoping problem. But that's like bringing an atom bomb to a pocket-knife fight. Price is one of the most powerful tools you have in a project conversation; use it effectively.

So what's the best way to solve for the lack of scope? Create one. Your clients look to you as the professional who can get them to a destination they can't reach on their own. You're the travel agent of their project, and you know exactly what tools and routes best take you there. No one pays a travel agent to lead them in circles, and that's what time-based rates give you permission to do: work without an end in sight.

Spend the time with your customer to learn about where they need to go, and why. If you can understand their desire for the destination, you can put together a few packages that get them excited about where they'll soon be—and make you rich at the same time.

Behold the light: you're ready for value-based pricing.

2

VALUE-BASED PRICING

I'M A SNEAKERHEAD. I've reduced the number of sneakers in my rotation in recent years; I'm down to about thirty pairs. Before I became a designer, I was a manager at Foot Locker, Inc., and its subsidiaries. As you can imagine, the then-50% discount was a blessing and a curse.

In sneaker culture, there's a phenomenon known as a *release*, the first day a well-known brand is set to sell a particular shoe. For the Jordan XVII release—the 17th model of basketball superstar Michael Jordan's footwear—I got to my store around 4 a.m. to prepare the stockroom. People would start lining up around 5 for the store to open at 8. And, they'd be prepared to spend up to $500 for a pair. Once the stores sold out, people could only get the sneakers from private dealers or eBay.

Now, I could go to any local big-box store and buy some molded rubber to cover my feet for less than $10, but something about these shoes made people want to spend twenty to fifty times more. The customers *valued* the sneakers. Some were collectors and couldn't pass them up. Some were brand loyalists. Some loved the aesthetic. Some appreciated the functionality; they were the best basketball shoes around. Whatever the motivation, people were willing to give up their money, time, and logic to get their hands on a pair (**FIG 2.1**).

Isn't that what we want in our businesses? Don't we want our clients to be so excited to work with us that they're willing to defy reason (within reason)? How do we get them to line up outside our metaphorical doors at the crack of dawn? You need to have something that's worth so much to them that they can't stand not having it.

You need to have something they value.

DEFINING VALUE-BASED PRICING

Here's the typical understanding of how a transaction works, and what it means for your bottom line. If you subtract your costs from the price you charge, the surplus is called *profit* (**FIG 2.2**).

FIG 2.1: The Nike Mag, a replica of the shoe featured in *Back to the Future Part II,* was only sold via auction. The highest bid was $9,959, on release day in 2011 (https://bkaprt.com/pd/02-01/). Photograph courtesy Nike (https://bkaprt.com/pd/02-02/).

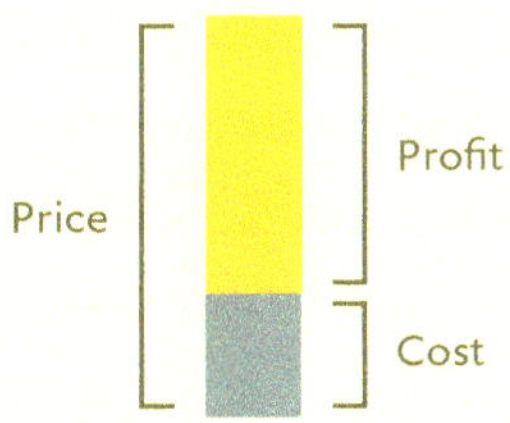

FIG 2.2: Profit is the difference between price and cost. Hope I'm not blowing any minds here.

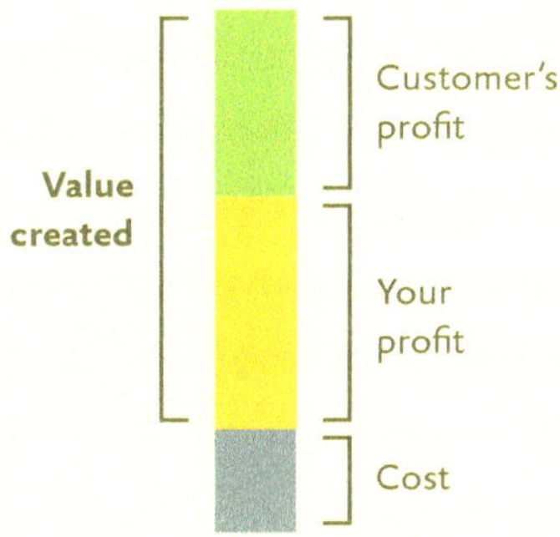

FIG 2.3: The secret in graph form: the more value you create, the more you increase your customer's profit as well as your own.

But every transaction has another kind of profit that most people forget about: the customer's profit. The combination of your profit and your customer's profit is called *value* (**FIG 2.3**).

I'm a huge believer in value, because it gets at what makes our work succeed (and yep, what makes us profit): a focus on what we can do for our customers. As web and app makers, we build our businesses on trading something valuable we have that customers want for something valuable they have. What they want includes the obvious: design, development, content strategy, information architecture, research. But it goes beyond services. Our clients long for heading home to their families earlier every night. More efficient workflows. Reduced overhead. Less stress. Pride in their products. These things hold value.

Your job as a service provider is to create as much value as possible for your customers.

The more you provide value for your clients, the more they profit. Their businesses do better, and they're happier. That's the backbone of value-based pricing—your primary driver is what you can achieve for your customers. The more profit—read: value—you can create for them, the more of that profit you're entitled to. Value-based pricing is the intersection of how much value you can create for a customer and the amount you ask for in return.

To ensure you can hold up your end of the bargain, you must first understand how valuable you are and what you value.

Your value

How valuable are you? (Or, for agency owners, how valuable is your agency?) For some, this can be a hard question to answer, buried under an avalanche of self-doubt, imposter syndrome, and other tragedies. We're all capable of creating value, but it might have been a while since you last believed that. Let's rebuild that instinct by looking at a few examples.

How much does a website cost?

Ask any proponent of value-based pricing, and they'll recite this mantra: price the customer, not the service. Building a website doesn't have an inherent price. My agency once designed and built a website for $18,000, and we did the same project for a different client for $230,000 that year.

A website doesn't have an inherent price. An illustration doesn't have an inherent price. Heck, a shoeshine doesn't even have an inherent price; you could get a fast shoeshine, a thorough shoeshine, a specific-type-of-shoe shoeshine...they have different prices because they're valuable in different ways to different people at different times. Price the customer, not the service or product.

I have a slight twist on that. As I'm pricing a customer, I can't help but think about another crucial part of the equation: me. How badly do I need this work? Perhaps this month, I'm booked up, and it would take quite a sum to persuade me to take on anything new. Next month, however, work may dry up, and I may be willing to do the project for much less. Same customer, but the timing changes things. For me, value pricing is even more than pricing the customer. It's about pricing the moment.

Object value pricing

When you start to assess your own value, it can feel awkward. It's like going to the gym again after months of couch surfing: even the shortest workouts make you sore. Keep at it. Pricing is a muscle. You need to keep exercising it to get stronger.

Let's say someone comes to you to design a website. What dollar amount do you put in a proposal? (Shrug emoji.) Money is tough, because it's little pieces of paper and some jingly coins. They're abstractions of value, and abstractions are tough to understand.

Here's an exercise you can do every time you get a new inquiry. I call it *object value pricing*. Don't think about money; instead, think about what object you would take in trade for the job. Would you do the website for a new camera? No way. What about a new MacBook Pro? Meh. A used Honda Accord? Maybe. Two years' worth of mortgage payments? Now we're talking.

You've got your range. A used Accord might be about $12,000. A $1,000/month mortgage accumulates to $24,000 over two years. So, this job feels somewhere between $12K and $24K for you. Do this exercise a few times and you'll trust your gut a lot more when it comes to recognizing what you're worth.

Ch-ch-ch-ch-changes

Your value isn't "set and forget." It changes constantly—annually, monthly, even daily.

The largest factor in your current value is *your ability to walk away from a prospect.* If your bank account is full, your portfolio is stacked, and you're incredibly fulfilled in the work you're doing, a prospective client would have to pitch *you* on taking their project. If you won't take their project for $10K, the only recourse they have is to offer you $20K, then $50K, then $100K, until you finally take it—or don't.

In social psychology, the *scarcity principle* says people put a higher value on an object or service that's scarce and a lower value on one that's abundant. When you're at Peak Valuablenessity™, the services you offer are at their scarcest, so you introduce maximum FOMO for your prospects.

On the flip side, if you're struggling to pay the bills and have no projects on deck, you take what you can get. The scarcity principle works both ways; in this scenario, *you're* the one anxious that the client—and their purse strings—will go elsewhere.

Whether you're slammed or scrambling, a set rate doesn't make sense. Let's say you have a rate of $100/hour (the industry standard). When you're at your most valuable—when you're most able to walk away—charging the same as everyone else doesn't do you any favors. It may even work against you: an industry standard price makes you seem less scarce than you actually might be.

When you're at your least valuable—when you really need the gig—you probably want to drop that rate lower than what everyone else is charging to be more competitive.

So what's a designer to do when a potential client asks what your rate is? Here's the script I follow:

Client: *What's your rate?*
Me: *I don't have one.*
Client: *So how do you know what to charge me?*
Me: *I'll spend as much time with you as I can to understand what you need and want. Based on what I hear, I'll come up with a few options that simultaneously seem like a steal for you and are*

lucrative for me. I want to make sure that we can both profit by working together.

Client: *That sounds wonderful. When do we start?*

Me: *We already have!*

See how easy that was? Being able to tailor each price to your value and what your client values is the beauty of value pricing, and it's one of most courteous things you can do for them.

As much money as possible

Perhaps the biggest misconception of—and objection to—value pricing is that it's about charging the largest amount of money possible.

Let me clear that up: it's not.

It's easy to think that way. After all, I use words like *value* and *premium* and *worth* all over this book. But value pricing is about making the price *match* the value. If the value of what you're doing is small, it's okay for the price to be small. If the value is immense, the price should follow suit.

Now that you have a few examples for assessing your own value, let's figure out the other side of the coin: What's it worth to your customer?

What your customer values

Esau and Jacob were twins. Esau was born a few minutes earlier, so he earned the inheritance of his family as the firstborn. (He was also his dad's favorite.) One day, he was out hunting and didn't catch anything. Hungry, he returned home, where generally jealous Jacob was cooking a stew. Big brother Esau asked for a bowl. And Jacob value-priced him: "I'll trade you this stew for your inheritance."

"What good is an inheritance if I starve to death? I'll take it!" Esau retorted.

What's a bowl of stew worth? A few bucks? A huge inheritance? The real answer is: it depends. Remember: price the customer, not the service. How badly do they want or need that service? How badly do they want or need that service *right now*? Even more than pricing the customer, value pricing is about pricing the moment.

The rush charge, the pain-in-the-butt charge, and more

When clients want it done yesterday, often our instinct is to jack up our hourly rates. That's a form of value pricing: your client's saying they value speed, and you're saying that speed is worth a premium. In practice, with hourly (or any time-based) rates, you bill less the faster you work. But customers that value speed would pay double for a project that gets done in half the time they expect—charge for that.

The same concept applies when a prospect seems difficult to work with. I leave it to you to do your personal calculus on what makes a project worth the hassle, but I do know people who tack an extra $10/hour to their standard rates. That's value pricing too: putting a price on tolerance.

In his excellent book *Pricing for Profit,* business consultant Dale Furtwengler lists other examples of value that clients are willing to pay for: friendliness, integrity, dependability, convenience, image, service, innovation, and knowledgeable salespeople. These are all things that you can—and should!—put a price on. (Furtwengler even demonstrates how to quantify these values into actual dollar amounts. While that's out of the scope of this text, I highly recommend giving his book a read.)

So what do you do when you get an inquiry from a prospective customer? How do you find out exactly *how* valuable the project is and which values are most important to them?

The questionnaire

This series of rapid-fire questions is designed to extract as much project detail as possible in a short period. The trick is to keep your ears open for value, not just the specifics of the answers. Here's what I ask, and what I'm listening for. (I typically email these questions first, and then follow up on the answers through a phone call.)

What's the timeframe? Does a certain event depend on this project launching?

Speed is a value. A big part of what your customers pay for is your expertise and your time to put that into practice for them. Customers who want something fast should be willing to pay accordingly—read: a lot—for that service.

Look out for customers who manufacture false urgency. "Our CEO wants it done by May" isn't a real deadline, but "We want this fantasy football app done two weeks before the season starts" is.

What are you looking for from us? Do you want us to design, build, and launch the whole site? Or do you have developers or other partners lined up and only need us for design?

You have to understand the actual scope of the project. This also answers how much the customer knows about you. Are they asking for what you do best? Do you even offer the services they want? Is it an opportunity to experiment with the things you'd like to offer but don't have much experience with?

This question gives you the chance to discover what else your customer's looking for. If they go into dreams of a more coherent social strategy, and you're talking websites, it's a good time to offer your other services—the classic up-sell, but done tastefully and appropriately.

Last, you can double-check their comments on timeline. Are they asking for six months' worth of work but only giving you six weeks to do it? That can show you how much your customer actually knows about the work they want. It's either a chance for you to demonstrate your expertise and steer the ship a bit more, or a warning sign that the expectations are misaligned and you're headed for troubled waters.

Have you already started on any part of the project? Do you have existing work? A new logo? Some rough designs or ideas for the site?

On the surface, it's good to know how much of a head start you'll have on work—or how much you'll need to undo. If the client already has a ton of wireframes and documentation, they may be looking for someone who can execute without questions instead of someone who can refine their vision. I'm wary of situations like this, because it becomes difficult to provide real value—and charge for it.

You might have more baggage to unpack in their answers. If they're shopping around because they fired their last agency, sure, maybe the agency didn't do good work. But it's also possible this organization doesn't know what they want, or they're overly demanding, and the agency quit because it was too much to deal with. Sniffing this out early will help you to make an informed decision on whether you want to inherit the work.

The answer isn't always bad. Through this question, I've also found that the customer was already working with an amazing branding, motion graphics, or development shop that I was dying to collaborate with. Surfacing those opportunities can make for better holistic work. But get a view of your customer's complete ecosystem of partners before proceeding.

How large is your team? What are the roles you envision on your end?

Team size says a lot about how much an organization values the project they're hiring you for. If the project will commandeer the entire marketing team's attention for a whole year, it's probably really important to them. However, if it's something they're sticking the new guy on because he has nothing else to do, the project probably isn't a priority—and they likely won't spend a lot either.

Large companies are especially notorious for starting projects and not paying proper attention to them, leading to project pauses and ultimately stagnation. You're looking to see if the team you're working with can build the right momentum on the project to actually ship it. Are they a group of middle managers who don't have the authority to finalize decisions? If the person who hired you is a high-ranking executive, will they have the availability to respond as quickly as you'll need them to, or will they be pulled in too many directions? I've often had to request certain roles on the client end (like project managers or supporting designers) to make sure our work gets put to good use.

You also get clues about certain stakeholders. Is there a VP who doesn't care about wireframes but will want to be involved heavily in the aesthetic phase? Does the technology director want to audit your markup at every round? Use this information to wisely scope and price the project. I don't recommend working with difficult customers, but if you do, don't forget the pain-in-the-butt surcharge.

How did you hear about our work? What specifically interests you about it? Any projects you're keen on?

This is a basic weed-out question. I get people who've never seen our work, thought we were a different agency, mistakenly sent us an inquiry, and lots more.

It's crucial to work with people who respect you and your work. If they don't know you from a hole in the wall, make like a tree and stop wasting your time.

Keep an eye out for generic terms or buzzwords, like clean! Simple! Modern! Responsive! They can either let you know that the customer hasn't spent much time with your work *or* reveal what's important to them as an end result.

How much money have you set aside for this project?

The million-dollar question. (Hopefully, literally!)

If you're not asking about money when you talk to a prospective client, you're doing it wrong. All of these questions unearth the value of a project, but this one is the most direct. Don't skip it.

(Notice that I asked about "money," not "budget." The word budget connotes cheap, like it's all you could afford—"not in the budget." Focusing on "money" keeps the conversation on maximum value, whereas "budget" draws attention to minimum spending.)

Lots of people are uncomfortable discussing money, so where this question falls in the order of all your questions is important. Ask too late, you'll look like you're too afraid to ask about it—awkward. Ask too early, you'll look like you're only in it for the cash—awkward. I've had the best results when I've placed this question about three-quarters of the way through, after I've lobbed them an easy one—why they thought to contact me. Bonus: that question perfectly lines me up to say I'm worth a premium.

The more comfortable you are talking about money, the more comfortable your client will be. It's your job to put them at ease through these questions, so treat this with the same straightforward attitude as you do team size and timeframe. This takes practice, so don't worry if you need a few tries to really nail it.

Many clients shy away from giving a number. They'll often counter your question with something like, "Well, we want to know how much you think it'll cost." Sometimes they honestly don't know. Most times, though, they have a number in mind and they're hoping you come in lower.

At this point, I'll use a technique that almost always works. Ask: "Are you aiming to spend closer to $500K, $50K, or $5K?" You're trying to force sticker shock to get a feel for a range.

Look for a gut reaction. You'll often hear something like, "Oh, definitely not $500K."

You politely reply, "Of course not! How do you feel about spending $50K?"

They say, "Yeah, if we can stick to about $50K, that'd feel right."

Voilà: you've got a starting point for your project price.

Are you talking to other companies about this project? Might we ask how many? What do you like about their work?

You just asked an awkward question about money—and got through it!—so you might as well lump the awkward questions together.

It's nice to know who you're up against. Being informed about your competition isn't just a sales tactic; it helps you to better serve your customers. Lots of studios have a design style; wouldn't it help you to know that your customer likes that style, especially if it's not your own?

Knowing the competitive landscape also helps you assess your chance of winning. If you're one out of twenty competitors, run! The odds aren't in your favor, or worse: your customer doesn't know what they want or how to make decisions. I've rarely entered situations where more than three studios were pitching.

Anything else we should know about?

The catch-all. Time for closing statements. Check that you haven't missed anything. Also, ask yourself if they're the type of client you'd have a meal with. If you can't hang out, what makes you think you'll be able to work together?

This is your last opportunity in this initial conversation to let your client know that you're listening. For example, if they say they're in a rush, let them know that you'll "turn around a proposal before the end of the week to get this moving." Or, if they seem hesitant about whether you can do the work they want because they don't see it in your portfolio, offer to immediately introduce them to a former client who can vouch for similar work. Projects where the client feels heard often end in success.

(If you want a text version of these questions to email to a client, grab them from GitHub: http://bkaprt.com/pd/02-03/).

ALIGNING VALUE

Imagine you're sitting at a blackjack table with your potential client, with the dealer across from you both. Instead of handing out cards, he gives you each a piece of paper. He asks your client to ignore all the cockamamie psychology of trying to get a deal and instead write down an honest dollar amount that they're willing to spend on the project. ("As little as possible" is not an appropriate response.) He asks you to ignore all the baloney of trying to milk as much money as you can and instead write down an honest dollar amount that you're willing to do the project for. ("As much as possible" is not an appropriate response.)

You each slide your paper back to the dealer, who glances at them. He flips them toward you so you can see what's written. Both pieces of paper have the same number: $10,000.

Congratulations: you've come to terms.

When your client was writing their number, they thought:

- They tried this project last year with an inexpensive—but inexperienced—freelancer. They paid $5,000; paying more might lead to better results.
- They might get their weekends back if the thing you build actually automates a lot of the work for their team.
- They'd be more than willing to spend half of their $20,000 annual budget for audience development in order to exceed the standing company record by 15%.
- Their colleague at that other company spoke highly of you and your work, which liberated that team from previous monotonous tasks.

These are all the things they value. They picked $10,000 to represent that value.

When you were writing your number, you thought:

- You're busy right now, and you'd have to turn away many inquiries to commit to this work.
- You're an expert on building plugins to automate content migrations from a print to a web CMS, which is exactly what this client needs. You've done similar work for some of the world's largest media companies, so few people can do this better than you.
- This work would take a month to do, because you can reuse tools you've built in the past. This would take anyone else three to six months.
- This client's team easily spends between $15,000 and $20,000 each month on meaningless tasks, just because their current system is inefficient.

- Your family needs $4,000/month to pay the bills and live comfortably.
- You'd like to specialize in this kind of project.
- You'd like working with this client, because the entire team seemed friendly and open to your ideas.

These are all the things you value. You picked $10,000 to represent that value.

The magic in pricing is when you can match what your customer values with how valuable you are. That's why you don't see a lot of students doing work for Fortune 500 companies: students aren't often capable of creating all the value that's possible. The balance of value is what makes for the most productive relationships; iron, after all, sharpens iron.

3

A PRICING CASE STUDY

HERE'S A REAL request for proposal (RFP) my design collaborative, SuperFriendly, fielded. (I've changed the names.) We'll use it to play out the full scenario, from receiving an inquiry to responding using value-based pricing.

Hello,

We are pleased to invite you to submit a proposal for front-end development of the AmericanBoatCompany.com redesign.

Mega Agency is the Agency of Record (AoR) for American Boat Company, and we are seeking a front-end partner to develop the next-generation user interface and presentation layer for AmericanBoatCompany.com.

The attached RFP provides the concrete business requirements and key evaluation criteria. We hope it provides you with valuable information about the project, context, and timelines, and enables you to submit your proposal. Your proposal should specifically address the needs outlined in the attached document.

Please note that proposals must be received by 12:00 a.m. EST on 7/14/14, and should be sent to Calvin UX Director (calvin@megaagency.com) and me. Project stakeholders and ABC Procurement will review the proposals, and announce their decision on 7/25/14.

If you have any questions, we would be happy to answer them in a conference call. Additionally, questions can be directed via email to Calvin and me.

We would appreciate a brief receipt confirming that you have received the RFP, and look forward to receiving your proposal.

Best,

Sally Producer

Even from the initial email, I'm looking for signs of value—what's important to the client, what's interesting about the project for SuperFriendly:

- Sally didn't address my company or me by name. I wonder if she has any idea about our work. I bet we're one of sixty companies invited to this RFP process.

- I'm well aware of American Boat Company. I've ridden on their boats, and this could be a really cool project. Plus, they're a Fortune 100, publicly traded company, so I can easily find a lot of their financial information to evaluate how much my work can—or can't—affect their bottom line.
- They mention front-end development, but nothing about design—my company's main strength. Will this project be a good fit? Maybe it's a job where they have Photoshop files and are only looking for the lowest bidder to slice and dice.
- I don't know Mega Agency. Let me look at their work. [*Looks*] Wow, I've seen a lot of their work before and didn't realize it. I need to find out if they're looking for an expert to partner with, or if they're expecting to dictate directions to a vendor that won't question anything.
- Two weeks to prepare a proposal. That's not too bad.
- No mention of spec work. Good.
- They're happy to have a conference call. Awesome. This isn't a "deposit your answers into this system" RFP. I'm hopeful that means we're pitching against a small number of firms, because they probably don't want to telephone sixty agencies.
- They're asking to confirm receipt of this email, which I don't often see in RFP inquiries. That's smart.

I'm not a fan of RFPs, because they usually come in the form of long documents that don't say much, but this one has enough substance to pursue it further. The project is valuable to me because it's prestigious, and Mega Agency may be great to work with. The project sounds like it's valuable to them because they need someone to do the work that they can't, but need to, for American Boat Company.

I pop open the attached document, a twenty-two-page brief that contains:

- Overviews of the companies involved (both agency and customer).
- The five phases of the project. Phases 1 and 2 are thoroughly documented, while Phases 3-5 look vague. Each phase lasts

about a quarter (Phase 5 is two quarters), so we're talking about an eighteen-month engagement.

- Lots of technical requirements (must use LESS and not Sass, lazy-loading guidelines, browser support requirements, etc.).
- Almost no design requirements.
- Expected deliverables and process info.
- Expected format for the RFP response.

A supplier survey, asking for financial information about my company (tax returns, annual revenue for the past three years, etc.).

I decide to email Mega Agency:

Hi Sally,

Thanks for getting in touch!

We'd absolutely love to help you and Mega Agency do great work for American Boat Company. However, we can't really do our best work under a rigid RFP process. We're different from a lot of other agencies, and a process that forces us to look the same as everyone else makes us look ... well, kinda the same as everyone else.

We'd love to chat about how we could create the most value for you, though admittedly some of it would be a bit outside the steps you've outlined. If that's not possible, we definitely understand, but regrettably will have to politely bow out.

Whaddya say? Would you have some time for us? If so, could we send over a few questions about the project that will queue us up for a good conversation?

I'm doing a few things here:

- I'm being honest. It's the best way to start any conversation or relationship.
- I'm reminding Mega Agency that we're different. Presumably, they contacted us because we stood out from the crowd.
- I'm establishing our ability to walk away. I don't need their work right now, so I'm looking for a reason to want it.

They reply:

> *We'd love to chat. We're excited to have you in the running and look forward to receiving your questions.*

Awesome. I've established that it's at least valuable enough for Mega Agency to spend time with me and my team to see if we align. But I don't yet know specifically *how* valuable, and I need to know before I can assign any numbers to anything. So I send my questions—see the questionnaire from Chapter 2—and get on the phone with Mega Agency. I learn:

- Mega Agency's team consists of strategists, UX designers, graphic designers, copywriters, an account manager, and a heavily involved chief creative officer (CCO). With agencies this size, the CCO often isn't involved unless it's an important account.
- I'm pitching against three other agencies. Mega Agency isn't willing to reveal who they are.
- They heard about SuperFriendly through a talk I did on responsive design processes—a good sign that my approach and subject matter expertise resonates with them.
- The October deadline lines up with the first media buy. It's not a fake deadline, and missing it can have some dire consequences for American Boat Company.
- They've been burned before by a vendor who wasn't available enough for their liking.
- They won't tell me how much or little they want to spend. (We'll come back to this.)
- Mega Agency has been working with American Boat Company for the last eight years and is ready to "take it to the next level."
- They say "best-of-breed" a gazillion times.
- I confirm that the project is development only, and they already have comps.

At this point, I pause the conversation. You can't make a site in a vacuum by throwing comps over the wall. I take this opportunity to demonstrate some expertise and put up a few roadblocks. I tell them that if they're after a chop shop, I'm probably way too expensive and others would be better; in fact, I'm happy to recommend some. But if they want best-of-breed, they'll need to be open to changing things around a bit. I share two stories of recent projects that were incredibly successful because of tight integration between the design and development teams. I offer to write a proposal that restructures their design process to get to their desired outcome. Essentially, I'll write a proposal for the job I want, not the job they're offering. They agree vigorously; I can all but hear them nodding over the phone.

Now I have enough to price the project.

QUANTIFYING VALUE

My go-to pricing framework is *Goldilocks pricing*: you offer clients three options (often tiered). This technique is effective because:

- It employs the *anchoring effect,* when the first element you encounter influences how you feel about every other price. In a TED talk, psychology and behavioral economics professor Dan Ariely described an anchoring experiment he did with MIT students, on the *Economist*'s subscription prices (http://bkaprt.com/pd/03-01/). At the time, the *Economist* listed three choices: $59 for web only, $125 for print, or $125 for both. Ariely surveyed a hundred students: which would they pick? Unsurprisingly, 84% chose both, with 16% opting for web only. He did a second survey, with another group of students—but he removed the print subscription. The results flipped: this time, 68% chose web only, while 32% chose both print and web. What Ariely found was that the inclusion of the print-only subscription, at $125, made the combo, also $125, feel like a deal—so more people picked it.
- Three options enable you to create your own framing. When you send over one price, your client has no choice but to compare you with other bids or the cost of similar services in the past. By listing multiple options with their own indi-

vidual prices, you encourage your client to compare you with you.

- Last, it forces you to think critically about *different* ways you can create value for your client. Exploring these options can lead you to unearth ideas you or your client may not have dreamed of otherwise.

One last note before we dig into the pricing proposal for Mega Agency. In brainstorming your options, the biggest mistake you can make at this stage is focusing on what type of deliverables you can create. You want to price on value to the client, which means you're selling results, not deliverables—as noted in Alan Weiss's book, *Value-Based Fees:*

> *Most consultants place their value proposition at the wrong end of the equation: they focus on their ability to do rather than on the client's ability to improve.*

When I'm pricing options, I base each one on a different trait or result that's important to the client. I then sort them into tiers: high value, medium value, and low value (**FIG 3.1**).

You may recall that Mega Agency wouldn't tell me how much they wanted to spend, which may happen to you from time to time, even if you use my magic sticker-shock question. That's okay: it gives you the opportunity to focus solely on the value you can provide in each of your options, rather than trying to come in at a number your client (maybe unrealistically) conjured. If you're new to pricing, getting a number is a great safety. But the more you price, the more comfortable you'll feel basing everything on the value you'll provide.

Option 1

Given everything I've heard from Mega Agency, I think they value **expertise** the most. That's what I'd like to sell as the first option. So, what's the price of expertise?

Before I set the price, I should determine what expertise Mega Agency would get. Well, they want the best responsive site possible. I've worked on some pretty great responsive sites,

OPTIONS	VALUE
Option 1	High
Option 2	Medium
Option 3	Low

FIG 3.1: A starter template for creating a range of options for your client.

if I do say so myself. I also collaborate with people and teams who make some of the best responsive sites out there, and teach others how to make them at conferences and in workshops—like Brad Frost, who creates great responsive resources; Paravel, who've done responsive projects for massive organizations like Microsoft; and heck, Ethan Marcotte, who invented the dang thing. What if I could get people like that to offer consulting time on this redesign?

The site would be good. *Really* good. It might win awards. That means it'd get talked about in books and magazines and conferences and interviews, both by the people who worked on it and by those who admired the work. That would probably get Mega Agency more attention and more work like it. And what would *that* bring in for Mega Agency? A few phone calls to agency friends with similarly sized accounts, combined with my own experience, tell me that similar agency-of-record work is worth about $8 million of revenue per year on average.

Based on those factors, it's reasonable to ask for 10% of their potential gain.

```
10% of $8,000,000 = $800,000
```

(I don't have any specific science on picking 10%, but I've found that around a tenth of the total potential bounty is both small enough for the client to consider a worthy investment and large enough to be lucrative for me.)

Since the project has five phases, I decide to offer a price of **$160,000/phase** for the expertise option (**FIG 3.2**).

```
$800,000 ÷ 5 phases = $160,000/phase
```

OPTIONS	VALUE	TYPE	PRICE
Option 1	High	Expertise	$160,000/phase
Option 2	Medium		
Option 3	Low		

FIG 3.2: High option done: the price of expertise is $160K/phase.

OPTIONS	VALUE	TYPE	PRICE
Option 1	High	Expertise	$160,000/phase
Option 2	Medium	Unlimited availability	$100,000/month
Option 3	Low		

FIG 3.3: Two down, one to go.

OPTIONS	VALUE	TYPE	PRICE
Option 1	High	Expertise	$160,000/phase
Option 2	Medium	Unlimited availability	$100,000/month
Option 3	Low	Deliverables	$400,000

FIG 3.4: All options filled in.

tOption 2

Mega Agency moderately values **unlimited availability**. To price this, let's revisit the value pricing rationale from Chapter 2.

Mega Agency wants to be able to call me anytime, and I'll be there for them. How much is it worth for me to be on call for a year? How much is it worth to turn down every other project because I'll have to be that dedicated?

In 2013, SuperFriendly grossed about $1 million. To get an exclusive for a yearlong project, they'd have to at least replace that income. That's $83,333.33/month, but I'll round up to $100,000 to make the math easier.

The price of option 2 is **$100,000/month** (FIG 3.3).

Option 3

I bet Mega Agency will get the least value by someone completing the bulk of the work, Phases 1 and 2. Basically, **deliverables**. Now, you might think, "No way they value deliverables only a little. All customers want deliverables!" Sorta. Though many customers start a conversation asking for deliverables, it's really because they don't know what to ask for. No one was born a client, and most don't even know what questions to ask. (If this sounds familiar, see Mike Monteiro's *You're My Favorite Client,* another great title from A Book Apart. Finish this book first, though.)

Customers aren't directly interested in deliverables; they're interested in what those deliverables can do for them and *their* customers. An InDesign file of a prescription label is just binary data, but the application of that file's contents may help someone properly take their medicine and save their life.

How much do Phases 1 and 2 cost? To me, this option feels like a subset of Option 1, because Mega Agency is invested in working with experts to finish Phases 1 and 2. They know how to build a website; this time around, they want a better site than one they can muster on their own.

Since Option 1 is $160,000/phase and Option 3 has two phases, I estimate $320,000 for this option. However, doing less work with a client is often less efficient than doing more, so I bump the price up to $400,000 to accommodate any complexity that arises from covering only two phases (FIG 3.4).

AN OPTION BY ANY OTHER NAME

The last step is my favorite: naming the options. "Option 1" won't inspire anyone to drop a quarter of a million dollars. You're selling here; add a little romance.

Seeing as this is for American Boat Company, let's draw on nautical names. Instead of "Option 1," let's call the expertise option "The Eclipse," the most luxurious yacht in the world. Option 2 becomes "The RMS Olympic," a World War I troopship remembered for its reliability. The third option is now "Steamboat Willie," which has connotations of just chuggin' along (the deliverables) as well as being an incredibly innovative film for its time (the expertise).

This give us a new chart (**FIG 3.5**).

PO-TAY-TO, TO-MAH-TO

You'll notice that each price has a different unit (per phase, per month, fixed price). That's intentional. You may object, "But how can the client compare these with one another? Or with other bids?" Well, they can't. And you don't want them to—not on price, anyway. You want your client to focus on the value, on the results. Everyone you're pitching against likely sent one quote (unless they read this book before you); you sent three. You're presenting them with three unique ways you could help. You're sending the message that you can do things no one else can. Pricing with these options puts you in a category of your own.

ONE. GAJILLION. DOLLARS?!

I've been fortunate to work with a stunning range of clients, from local printing companies and tiny churches to giant corporations with multibillion-dollar revenues, and everything between. Perhaps the most valuable lesson I've learned is that they're all the same. People spend money the same, whether it's a few hundred dollars they've managed to stash away or it's a

OPTIONS	VALUE	TYPE	PRICE	NAME
Option 1	High	Expertise	$160,000/ phase	The Eclipse
Option 2	Medium	Unlimited availability	$100,000/ month	The RMS Olympic
Option 3	Low	Deliverables	$400,000	Steamboat Willie

FIG 3.5: Last step: name those options so they provide more of an emotional hook.

corporate checkbook. Spending 150% of the expense account is just as precious for a regional grocery store as it is for a Silicon Valley startup backed by venture capital. And I've produced equally valuable results for both types of clients; ask any other experienced pricer, and they'll tell you the same story.

Let me assure you that this isn't only an approach for big companies with big bank accounts, and it's effective whether you run a big design shop or you're just starting out. It transcends dollar amounts: focusing on value scales better than any other method you can come up with. No matter your situation or your kind of client, these pricing techniques still apply—and will work wonders for you.

WRAPPING UP

With your prices set and a solid rationale to back them, you're ready to drop them into your proposal. While I won't get into the specifics of writing a great proposal—that's another book entirely—make sure you're clear about what you're offering and, whenever possible, walk your customer through their options on the phone or in person, never solely through email.

4

VALUE PRICING: WHAT TO EXPECT

I BET you're dying to know which option Mega Agency picked.

After we discussed all three, they thanked me and said they'd send an answer. Here's what I received:

> *Hi Dan,*
>
> *First off, let me tell you that we really loved your proposal. We knew when we selected you as a candidate that we'd be in for something different and exciting, and you did not disappoint. We were genuinely delighted by your response and had many a spirited discussion as we contemplated how we thought the project would unfold within the context of a partnership with you and your SuperFriends.*
>
> *You provided several very interesting options that gave us pause and got us looking at our project at a fundamental level. Unfortunately, we don't believe that this is the right engagement, or, more accurately, the right point in time in this project to bring you into the process.*
>
> *That said, the whole team agrees that we were thoroughly impressed with your presentation, approach, and candor when discussing the creative and technical aspects of the project and would absolutely love the opportunity to work with you in the future, preferably on a project where we can get you involved from square one.*
>
> *Thank you so much for your time and effort in preparing your proposal. It was appreciated and certainly opened our minds to some very interesting possibilities for the future.*
>
> *Best regards,*
>
> *Calvin UX Director*

What?! You mean to say I spent the whole previous chapter walking you through options for a project I didn't win?!

Yep.

Since I've started using value pricing, my loss rate on proposals has gone way up—my agency lands significantly fewer projects than when we had a standard hourly rate. (But we make way more money now.) Value pricing is scary, both for you as the provider and for the customer. It requires trust on both sides. It's risky for both parties.

You're not going to be right for every client. Not every client is going to be right for you. Value pricing helps bring that to light more quickly, because it forces you to think deeply about whether or not you can bring value to the table. Value pricing usually isn't for customers who want to rush into things. And it's not helpful if all you're interested in is running the meter as soon as someone calls you.

When you do find the client who believes in the value you can offer them, and you can confidently create that value, you will both profit tremendously.

My goal was to build a relationship with Mega Agency, even at the expense of a project. Since I've switched to value pricing, I haven't been selected for a few hundred projects I've submitted proposals for. Only one of those rejections has involved an objection to price.

Look again at Calvin's email. There isn't one word about price. The options I sent made Mega Agency reexamine the project at a fundamental level. (I'm adding value without even being hired yet.) They realized this project wasn't a good fit. Isn't that what we strive for with our work? To find clients we mesh well with? When's the last time a client sought you out and then realized it wasn't a fit before the project began? Most times, we discover this in the middle of the work, after each party has invested blood, sweat, and tears.

If you're going to lose a project, this is the way to do it: when a customer says, "We see the value. This isn't the right thing, but we'll be back." You know what? They came back, and you won't believe what happens next. (Buy our next book!)

Be as intentional about your pricing as you are with your design process, your GitHub repository, the clothes you wear to that meeting, your Photoshop layers, and every other part of your business. You've already proven that you're worth every penny you believe you are. Now you know how to go out there and ask for it.

RESOURCES

Books

- *Implementing Value Pricing,* Ronald J. Baker
- *Management Challenges for the 21st Century,* Peter F. Drucker
- *Positioning for Professionals,* Tim Williams
- *Predictably Irrational,* Dan Ariely
- *Pricing for Profit,* Dale Furtwengler
- *Pricing with Confidence,* Reed K. Holden and Mark R. Burton
- *Value-Based Fees,* Alan Weiss
- *The Win without Pitching Manifesto,* Blair Enns
- *Work for Money, Design for Love,* David Airey

Courses and coaching

- The Designer's Pricing Class, nuSchool, http://bkaprt.com/pd/05-01/
- Expensive Problem, Jonathan Stark, http://bkaprt.com/pd/05-02/
- Value-Based Pricing, Sean McCabe, http://bkaprt.com/pd/05-03/

Podcasts

- *Art of Value,* http://bkaprt.com/pd/05-04/
- *The Businessology Show,* http://bkaprt.com/pd/05-05/
- *Touring Implementing Value Pricing,* http://bkaprt.com/pd/05-06/

Websites

- Agency Compensation & Pricing, Ignition Consulting Group, http://bkaprt.com/pd/05-07/
- Breaking the Time Barrier, Mike McDerment and Donald Cowper, http://bkaprt.com/pd/05-08/
- Harvest Field Guide to Pricing, http://bkaprt.com/pd/05-09/
- Project Questionnaire, http://bkaprt.com/pd/05-10/

ACKNOWLEDGMENTS

First and foremost, thank you, God, for your incredible blessings and for the opportunity to share what you've given me with the world.

To Mom: thanks for showing me how to be calm, cool, collected, and uncompromising when people are cruel. To Dad, the coolest CFO I know: thanks for teaching me about balance and how to save money wisely. To my brother Jonny: thanks for lending me money to buy comic books and video games when I didn't follow Dad's advice about saving wisely.

Thanks to the amazing A Book Apart team, who graciously let me make this book with them. To Jeffrey Zeldman: thanks for letting me ride along with you for over a decade (!) through Happy Cog, A List Apart, An Event Apart, and now A Book Apart. I owe a great deal of my career to your kindness and generosity. To Katel LeDû: thank you for making it your mission to help me write the book that I wanted to write, and for reminding me to do so. To Tina Lee: thank you for showing me how to respect my readers by writing for them, not at them. To Mike Monteiro: thank you for writing such a fantastic foreword. To Lisa Maria Martin: thank you for your stellar copyediting and for rightly challenging the ideas that needed to be stronger. To Jason Santa Maria and Rob Weychert: thank you for making this book look sparkly and shiny. I'm honored to have been able to look over your shoulders for the last eleven years.

To Jervis Thompson: thank you for teaching me how to teach. To Jason Blumer: thank you for what you've done, as a CPA and a coach, for my business. Without you, SuperFriendly would still be "something I'll get around to one of these days." Thanks for asking me to start Businessology with you. Those conversations sparked many ideas in this book.

And finally, to my wife, Emily, and my daughters, Siddalee and Charlotte: thank you for everything. I value you above all else.

REFERENCES: PRICING DESIGN

Shortened URLs are numbered sequentially; the related long URLs are listed below for reference.

Chapter 1

01-01 http://www.aiga.org/calculating-a-freelance-rate

01-02 http://blog.teamtreehouse.com/calculate-hourly-freelance-rates-web-design-development-work

01-03 http://www.howdesign.com/design-business/pricing/hourly-rates/

01-04 http://adage.com/article/agency-news/4a-s-top-york-advertising-creatives-charge-750-hour/139409/

Chapter 2

02-01 http://www.nicekicks.com/2011/09/19/nike-mag-auction-2011-final-numbers/

02-02 http://news.nike.com/news/nike-mag-2015

02-03 https://gist.github.com/danielmall/87e4a93fa83f09e4ed18

Chapter 3

03-01 https://www.ted.com/talks/dan_ariely_asks_are_we_in_control_of_our_own_decisions

Resources

04-01 http://thenuschool.com/the-pricing-class/

04-02 https://expensiveproblem.com/

04-03 https://seanwes.com/value-based-pricing/

04-04 http://artofvalue.com/show/

04-05 http://www.businessology.biz/

04-06 http://www.verasage.com/blog/new-verasage-podcast-a-tour-through-implementing-value-pricing/

04-07 http://www.ignitiongroup.com/category/agency-compensation-and-pricing/

04-08 http://www.freshbooks.com/breaking-the-time-barrier

04-09 https://www.getharvest.com/field-guides/pricing/

INDEX

ABOUT THE AUTHOR

Dan Mall is a creative director and advisor from Philly. He's the director of SuperFriendly (superfriend.ly), a design collaborative that brings exquisite creative direction and design to the world's most important and interesting organizations. Dan is an enthralled husband and dad, and cofounded Typedia (typedia.com) (an encyclopedia for typefaces) and Businessology (businessology.biz) (a podcast and workshop series teaching designers how to run better businesses). He writes about design and other issues on Twitter (@danielmall) and on his industry-recognized site, danielmall.com.

9

A BOOK APART

WRITING FOR DESIGNERS

SCOTT KUBIE

FOREWORD BY
DAN BROWN

BRIEFS

Publisher: Jeffrey Zeldman
Designer: Jason Santa Maria
Editor-in-Chief: Katel LeDû
Managing Editor: Lisa Maria Martin
Copyeditor: Katel LeDû
Proofreader: Mary van Ogtrop
Book Producer: Ron Bilodeau

ISBN: 978-1-937557-79-9

A Book Apart
New York, New York
http://abookapart.com

TABLE OF CONTENTS: WRITING FOR DESIGNERS

FOREWORD

PLAYING THE PIANO WELL requires more than just technical skill, more than learning to press the right keys at the right moments. It also requires learning how to practice—that is, developing the habits to internalize those technical skills.

The same is true for words. Assembling them in just the right way takes practice. The book you're about to read isn't a guide for putting words together; it's a guide for how to *practice* writing. It's a manual for cultivating good writing habits.

Writing is a process, one that's difficult to articulate precisely. It's equal parts instinct and rote procedure, and Scott helps us navigate both. Like any good recipe, *Writing for Designers* is never definitive, immutable, or exhaustive. It's a starting point, overflowing with tools, techniques, and myriad ways to approach each step in the writing process.

Our design process is fraught with words: words are used to document our ideas, to plan usability tests, to validate color choices. Words are used to prompt, cajole, warn, alert, explain, instruct, and reassure our users. They're an essential building block in the user experience, and we, as designers, can't ignore their power.

Writing for Designers will help you get more comfortable wielding that power in your design process. From getting version control right to tapping into your most creative self, let Scott show you the art and practice of writing.

—Dan Brown

INTRODUCTION

SHIT. THE WRITING. We forgot about the writing. The thing, the design thing...it needs words! Oh man, so many words. I thought somebody...wasn't the client going to...shit. We've got to get the writing done. We've got to get the writing done! How are we going to get the writing done?!

Don't worry, friend. I'm here. We'll get the writing done. The first step is to accept a hard truth: *someone* has to do the writing.

Some teams seem to build their whole process around *not* writing. They fill wireframes with *lorem ipsum* (that fake Latin text that confuses stakeholders) and write *CTA goes here* on their buttons. I've been handed my share of comps where anything remotely word-based was represented by a bunch of squiggly lines.

You know that comic about how to draw an owl? Step one: draw some circles. Step two: draw the rest of the fucking owl. That's you with your squiggly lines. Rude.

Everything left unwritten is a mystery box of incomplete design. These mysteries beget other mysteries, and pretty soon you've got dozens of screens of things that kinda-sorta-*maybe* make sense but none of them can really be final because *you never wrote the words.*

Choosing words and *writing* what appears in an interface forces us to name components, articulate choices, and explain things to the user. It's part of design.

We know this, don't we? We knew it at the beginning of the design project, and yet here we are. Why did we wait?

Writing is part of design

Words are one of the most *powerful* design materials available. They convey deeply complex meanings in a compact space. They load fast. They're easy to manipulate and easy to transmit. And the best part is, you don't have to invent any of them! You just have to use them.

Sometimes words get written off (see what I did there) as mere "details" in our designs. True details can wait until the end of your design process. Words, however, are deeply integrated throughout the user's experience of your design. Look at your favorite app, site, or interface. Take all the words away and what do you have? Not much!

Even if the particular thing you're designing seems light on words, take a broader view and you'll find words hiding everywhere:

- error messages and recovery flows
- confirmation screens
- user-visible metadata like page titles and search engine descriptions
- transactional emails
- in-app user assistance
- support documentation
- changelogs
- feature descriptions and marketing copy

These are as much a part of the design as the layout, graphics, and animations. Designs *depend* on words.

Even if your design were simple, beautiful, and intuitive, writing can take it one step further. Writing can reinforce how you want users to think about your design. Writing can explain the approach or philosophy that underpins your design. Writing can guide users through complex processes. Writing can even help cover for the quirks and compromises in our designs—hopefully not our first resort, but valuable nonetheless.

Sometimes the writing isn't done because we're trying to solve everything with "pure design." Supposed UX thought leaders throw around baloney like "Good design doesn't need explanation" and "If you have to use words, you've failed." Come on. I hope my pilot knows what all those switches in the cockpit do, but I also hope they're labeled, just in case.

To keep things simple in this book, we'll be talking about three general categories of writing you might have to do to support your design work:

- **Interface copy:** Often referred to as UI copy or microcopy, this is the text that's *deeply* integrated within the interface, like labels for form fields, text on buttons, navigation labels on a website, error messages, and similar. It's often made of single words or short phrases. If the interface would "break" or be extremely hard to use if you removed this text, we'll call it interface copy.

- **Product copy:** Writing that's integral to the function of the site/product/app/experience, but not necessarily a direct part of the interface—the body of an onboarding email, for instance, or a description of updates to an application in a changelog. This is content focused on helping/supporting the reader.
- **Marketing copy:** Longer-form writing that is primarily filling a sales or promotional sort of role. This is content focused on persuading the reader.

Depending on your product and organization, you might have many more buckets of content, or you may find the lines especially blurry even between these three. That's okay! These buckets will just make things easier while we talk about writing in this book. Cool? Cool.

(Oh, and "copy" is just a way to distinguish words written by a designer from the more generic idea of "text," which could be just about anything in your system, including user-generated input.)

Writing is always hard

If you know someone who makes writing look easy, you're right. They make it *look* easy. You can't plan well for a difficult journey if you assume it's going to be an easy journey. Accepting that writing is hard is an important step toward making it easier and getting it done.

Writing is hard because it's personal. Even if you're writing about something you don't feel strongly about, or even something you disagree with, it's still *your* writing. The words you write carry a little echo of you. To get the writing done, you're going to have to be a little vulnerable. Maybe a lot.

Writing is even hard for writers—and since most people don't realize that, they make it even harder on writers. They don't give writers enough time to write. They don't provide enough information to work with. They say things that minimize the difficulty of the task and the skill required to complete it. "You're so creative! This should be easy, right? Shoot me something back before lunch." Ugh.

Unfortunately, there's no special potion you can take to help you get the writing done, and even the most beautifully retro hipster typewriter still needs *you* to operate the keys.

Workflow gets the writing done

So if magic won't help you get the writing done, what will? In design contexts, a useful way to think about writing is *workflow*. Workflow is a big-picture idea that accommodates all kinds of different processes, techniques, and tools.

If following a recipe is a process, making dinner is a workflow. A dinner-making workflow has obvious phases—plan the meal, prep the ingredients, mix and cook things, finish and serve the meal. The specific steps and outcomes vary depending on the meal, but the basic workflow remains the same.

This is also a useful way to think about design writing. No matter what you're cooking up—no matter how custom the request and how many dietary restrictions your stakeholders might have—you'll follow the same basic workflow each time you do the writing:

1. Prepare (to write)
2. Compose (the words)
3. Edit (what you wrote)
4. Finish (the damn writing)

Planning your workflow means choosing the tools, techniques, people, and processes that will be part of each of these four phases. Until this framework becomes old hat, I recommend explicitly planning your writing workflow. Planning is how you avoid getting stuck. You might not immediately know every single tool, step, and person you'll need to get the writing done. But knowing even a few things, and giving yourself a basic map to follow to get the writing done, will help you learn what's missing.

WRITING WORKFLOW PLANNER

ASSIGNMENT	PROJECT	WRITER(S)
upgrade flow copy	Premium app updates	C. Boyle

PREPARE

TOOLS/STEPS/PROCESSES	INPUTS & SMEs	SCOPE / DEADLINE(S)
- design kickoff meeting - review XYZ corp upgrade flows - annotate wireframes w/ ID numbers for req'd messages - character limits from dev team	- project brief - marketing brainstorm meeting notes - original registration flow - Holt: product mgr.	SCOPE full UI text for sign-up flow (screens 2.4–5.3) DEADLINE(S) design review on 9/9

COMPOSE

TOOLS/STEPS/PROCESSES	WRITING ENVIRONMENT
- rough-in messages in dupe of design comps (Sprint 2 hrs Tuesday PM?) - rewrites for length - write full flow & review w/ Amy	Axure + TextMate

EDIT

VERSION CONTROL / FOCUS	TOOLS/STEPS/PROCESSES
VERSION CONTROL increment drafts in TextMate sync to private repo FOCUS TBD	- bring comps to design crit - edit against controlled vocabulary - schedule 30m w/ writing help desk

FINISH

TOOLS/STEPS/PROCESSES	PROOFING/QA	FINAL APPROVAL(S) / DESTINATION
- copy strings to production - update product inventory - design review	- have Amy dummy check - text file to QA team	FINAL APPROVAL(S) text: Holt implementation: QA DESTINATION email reference comps and text file to Terry, CC Holt

FIG 0.1: A structured worksheet can help you plan your writing workflow before you start, and serve as an anchor in the storm throughout the project. If you go this route, I recommend customizing it to suit the particulars of your organization.

Planning your workflow doesn't need to be a long process—or even something you share with other people. You can create a formal, structured worksheet to plan it out (**FIG 0.1**), you could sketch it out on a whiteboard or in a notebook (**FIG 0.2**), or simply make some notes at the top of a new document. The important thing is to think about *how* you're going to get the writing done before you start writing.

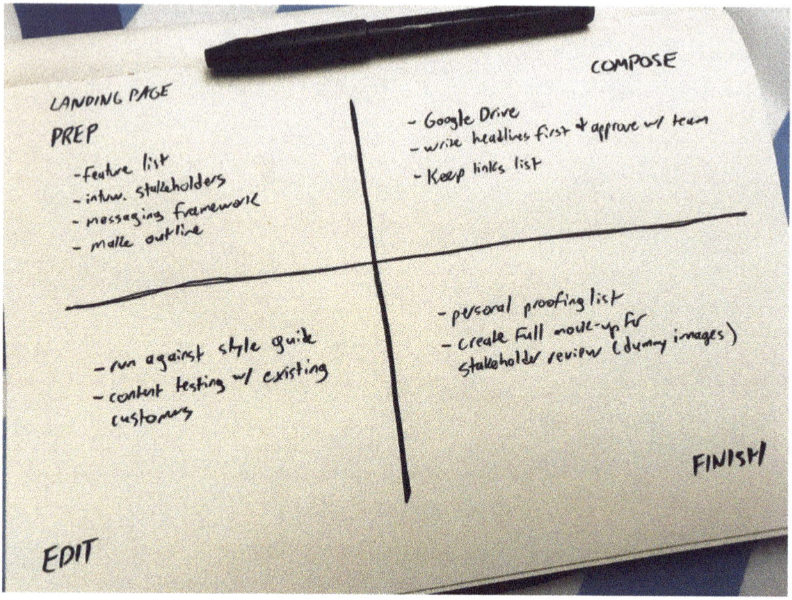

FIG 0.2: Planning your workflow on paper doesn't have to take long, and it's a nice break from staring at screens. Plus, you can cross things off as you go! (Always satisfying.)

You can write

Mr. Hays, my high school choir teacher, was a great recruiter. When he'd ask people to try out for choir, they'd protest with some version of "Oh, no, I can't sing." Nonsense, he'd say: "If you can talk, you can sing. It's all the same muscles!" And, more often than not, he'd pull that student right over to a piano and demonstrate to them that they could, in fact, sing.

In case you're skeptical, worried, or unsure about whether or not you can handle this, here's my pitch for writing: writing is just thinking plus typing. You can think. You can type (or otherwise get text into a computer). So yes, you can write.

We're going to get into all kinds of methods about how to compose and refine text throughout this book. But at the end of the day, writing is just thinking plus typing. Have some thoughts in your head, then write them down. Do this over and over until the writing is done. Every other tip, trick, method, and process is just an improvement or distillation of this basic approach.

And more good news: writing is more like design than you might think. Common design activities like framing the problem, identifying constraints, and exploring solutions are part of writing, too. Many of the methodologies one might use in UX work can be part of a writing workflow: stakeholder interviews, user research, content auditing, ideation workshops, critiques, and more.

Writing is always hard, yes. But it gets easier.

Good? Good. We're making progress already. It's time to Prepare.

1

PREPARE

THERE'S MORE TO WRITING THAN WRITING, especially when it's part of design. It's easier to get the writing done when you thoughtfully and intentionally *prepare* to do the writing. Smart writers do prep work on every assignment. You can be smart, too!

Whether you've got just a few strings to write for a new screen in your app, or a whole site full of marketing content, you'll want to do each of the following in order to fully prepare to get the writing done:

- articulate the assignment
- collect inputs
- generate ideas
- create structure
- make space to write

You might be feeling an instinct to rush past this phase, especially if you need those words, like, yesterday. But the more time you're able to spend here, the faster and more successful the remaining phases of your writing workflow will be. As Abraham Lincoln once said to Albert Einstein at Mark Twain's birthday party: If you've only got six hours to chop down a cherry tree, spend five hours sharpening your samurai sword. (I think that's the quote, anyway.)

ARTICULATE THE ASSIGNMENT

How are you supposed to get the writing done if you don't know what needs doing? What kinds of words? Where? For what purpose? What will it mean to be *done* with the writing? And what's your role in all this, anyway?

To answer these questions, you need to articulate your *writing assignment*. A design could require one big writing assignment, or lots of little ones. (Or lots of big ones. Or a mix!) The assignment is a flexible unit that says, "Here are the boundaries of the writing work I am responsible for."

Design writing assignments vary, of course, but tend to share some common characteristics:

- **Deadline**: When does the writing assignment—independent of the rest of the design project—need to be completed? This deadline could be something you work into the overall project plan, along with a schedule for check-ins and reviews.
- **Roles:** Your whole team needs a shared understanding of what it means to be the writer. What resources are available to writers? What expectations apply to writers? Are you responsible for getting a draft together for someone else to refine, or do you need to fully own the text? Take nothing for granted, especially the first time.
- **Context**: Where will the writing go? Who will be reading it? What are the circumstances of their reading it? You may feel like you know all of this from the design work already, but often a particular bit of writing (like an error message or confirmation dialog) will be specific to a subset of users or situations.
- **Requirements/Constraints**: What specific requirements and constraints apply to this writing? Are there character limits? Things that have to be mentioned for legal or practical reasons? Controlled vocabularies for interface elements?
- **Scope**: Scope is the checklist of all the "stuff" you have to actually write. Scope could be as simple as a description of the page and an outline of points you need to make, or it could be a complex inventory of messages required by an interactive experience.

Taken together, your deadline, role, context, requirements, and scope will give you a complete idea of what you need to do to be *done*. That's your assignment.

Err on the side of capturing this information publicly, even if it seems like no one else cares, just to cover your butt. The header area of a task or ticket in your project management system is a great option, or even just an email to your team: "Hey friends, here's what I understand about the writing needs on this project. Let me know if I've missed anything..."

This is a good gut-check moment. Does the assignment seem right? Good? Doable? In articulating your assignment, you might have already learned that what seemed like one assignment could be better managed as several. Or that the scope is just too darn big given the deadlines you need to hit. Do what you can to work out these kinks *before* you start writing to save time for everyone (but mostly you).

COLLECT INPUTS

Writing in design can feel more like assembling a puzzle than writing a novel—and someone's ripped open twenty puzzles at once and dumped all the pieces together. Worry about sorting and choosing the right pieces later. First, just make sure you *have* all of the pieces. You want to collect *inputs*.

If the people asking you to do the writing are not writers, they may not have any idea what would be useful to you. And you might not know what's useful until you see it. Ask stakeholders for all of the material they have relating to the project, even if they're not sure it's relevant.

At my company, we call this the "document dump." And sometimes it's a real dump, all right. But every junk yard has its treasures. Some good stuff to ask for:

- notes from meetings, interviews, and workshops
- project briefs and scope of work documents
- design comps, wireframes, and task flows
- marketing collateral
- user personas and research findings

If you know early on that you're going to be the writer on a project, take a fresh look at the calendar for any meetings or research sessions that might be valuable to sit in on. Many teams don't think to invite writers to these things. Being there in person (and doing your own interviews, if you have time) allows you to record what people actually say and how they say it—there's often a lot of flavor in how people speak that doesn't make it into a project manager's notes, but can be very valuable when it comes to doing the writing.

As you collect all of these things, be sure to keep your receipts. Track your inputs and where they came from. For a huge project with lots of inputs, you could go full spreadsheet, but descriptive file names and a few notes scribbled here and there might be enough. Later on in the project, you'll be grateful to have a paper trail, so to speak, as reviewers and stakeholders start asking questions and trying to poke holes in your writing. (It's okay—that's their job!)

Tracking inputs is especially important if you're able to reuse text that's already been through things like legal and compliance reviews. Two of the questions you'll hear most often about writing are: "Who else has looked at this?" and "Where did this [copy/phrase/slogan/benefit/feature/wording] come from?"

GENERATE IDEAS

Now we're closing in on where most people start their writing work—coming up with ideas. It's important to separate the action of generating ideas from doing the writing: first think, then write.

When you're generating ideas, anything is possible. The words are made up and the rules don't matter! This open mindset is necessary for creativity to flourish, as you've probably found in your design work. Treating the words in your design like annoying tasks that are in your way is not a mindset that lends itself to thoughtful, useful, and/or creative writing.

There are lots of ways to generate ideas for design writing. Some are going to work very well for your assignment, and some might not fit at all. I'm going to cover a few methods that work well in many situations.

Mindmapping

Most writing tools don't make thinking easy. When writers start generating ideas inside a blank document in Microsoft Word, or a blank body field in their CMS, they're literally doing their thinking inside of a box.

FIG 1.1: Marketing and product content often present many different paths for communicating the same idea. A mindmap encourages you to capture those options as they occur to you and keep moving, rather than debating them in your head.

Mindmapping breaks you out of that box. A mindmap is a visual outline that offers a flexible, nonlinear way of brainstorming and organizing your thoughts. You may have found yourself intuitively creating a mindmap when standing in front of a whiteboard or while scratching out ideas on a napkin.

For marketing and product content, mindmaps are great for transitioning from a big mess of ideas into a linear outline. You can start mashing together snippets of writing, recycled text, quotes, and any other random notion you have into one single canvas and begin sorting them into sections that make sense (**FIG 1.1**). For interface content, mindmaps can be a great way to collect and sort ideas for labels and feature names (**FIG 1.2**). In either case, having a bunch of options collected in one place ensures you'll never experience blank-page paralysis when it's time to do the writing.

Mindmapping makes it easy to start thinking and planning with words in small ways, without committing to *writing* everything at once, like that big, empty New Document window wants you to do.

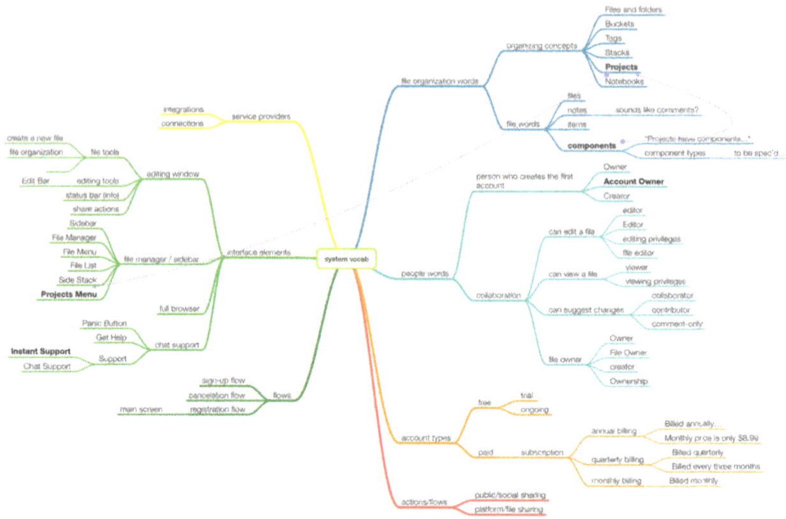

FIG 1.2: Mindmaps can help you make sense of the shape of an interface or workflow, or quickly collect a lot of label options.

Freewriting

Like mindmapping, freewriting is a technique you've probably informally used before. Freewriting is stringing words together for a *set amount of time*. It's especially effective for longform product and marketing copy.

If you want to try freewriting, here are a few things to consider:

- Use a timer, not a clock. If you're watching the clock, you're multitasking. The whole point of this is to *not* multitask—just write.
- Go for quantity, not quality. Try to write as many gosh-dang-doodily words as you can. Typitty type type type, my friend. Remember, this is still just an input—*not* a first draft.
- Fight the urge to switch to planning/designing/outlining. Write down whatever comes into your head, e.g., "Another reason this product is great is that—you know what, I need

to pick up milk from the store—is that it does XYZ faster than the competition." You can pull out the relevant bits to your outline later.

Here's an example of my freewriting for a to-do list application's marketing page:

we want you to subscribe to our to-do list software. we want your money please subscribe. go for the premium plan because it's the best value, especially if you sign up for a year. there's also a free forever plan for one device. it's very good software and it gets updated all the time, unlike the other guys who seem to only do a big update every six months. It syncs faster and more reliably than any other app (is that true?). encryption is coming soon and will be added for free when it releases. What are the benefits though how are we different, it's different because you can sync through whatever service you want, it allows you to customize how tags and categories work or not use them at all (it's to-dos done your way? tagline?)

Obviously—hopefully!—this is not website-ready marketing copy. Even if you cleaned up the sentences, it's still a big blob of text. That's okay—you're just generating ideas. This is a lump of wet clay, and you haven't yet decided if you're going to throw it into one big, beautiful vase or a set of ten tiny teacups.

You can even modify this technique for interface and conversational content with a few simple prefixes:

A: What do you want to do today?
B: ummm i want to buy pants I guess.
A: pants are a thing that we sell. see where it says PANTS up there?
B: Pants, got it. Wow that's a big list.
A: Yes. we sell many kinds of pants. Do you want men's or women's pants? Or maybe a certain color?
B: Black pants.
A: Here are all of our black pants.
B: Wow that is a lot of pants. Just show me women's pants.
A: Just women's pants, got it.

And so on. There are other techniques that will create similar inputs—having users talk aloud during user research sessions, for instance, or pair writing with a partner. Riffing like this can give you a lot to work with when it comes time to distill it down into tidy text for your interface.

Brainstorming

Let's be real: a brainstorming meeting is a meeting where everyone is responsible for generating ideas, which also means that *no one* is responsible for generating ideas—so avoid them if you can.

If there's too much organizational inertia working against you, and you find yourself stuck holding a "Let's brainstorm the writing!" meeting, these tips will make it less painful and more productive:

- Make idea generation the *sole* agenda item. Packing brainstorming into an existing agenda is asking for trouble. It takes a certain amount of time and energy to get into an open frame of mind—anything other than idea generation will pull you closed, hampering both the quantity and quality of your ideation session.
- Avoid decisions of all kinds. Decision-making is a form of convergent thinking. It's an act of limiting, reducing, filtering, choosing—*editing*. Making decisions, even small ones, brings the scent of criticism and closed-mindedness into the room that can spoil an otherwise productive brainstorming session.
- Encourage note-taking. If quantity is the goal—and it should be—forcing people to wait for a turn to speak, or to wait for the facilitator to write it on the whiteboard, is an agonizingly slow way to go about things. If you're concerned about people keeping ideas to themselves, try handing out sticky notes or index cards for notes to be periodically collected and added to a shared display.

CREATE STRUCTURE

To get the writing done, you'll need a clear *structure* to support your writing work. You'll want to turn your assignment into a to-do list of sorts that helps you see what kind of *writing*-writing work actually needs to happen.

There are three documentation structures that can guide your next phase: outlines, templates, and inventories.

Outlines

Outlines are great for longform writing like product overviews, knowledge base articles, in-product documentation, and so on. Outlines give an...uh...well, an outline of what you need to communicate and the rough order in which you need to communicate it.

Creating an outline may give you flashbacks to school research papers, but they are very useful in the world of design writing. Outlines are hierarchical: main point, sub-point, sub-sub-point (**FIG 1.3**). In that way, the outline not only informs your writing, but also the design—the big idea becomes your H1, the next level your H2. Blocks of similar ideas at the same level might work well as bullet points or a chart.

List out the main beats, the big ideas, of what you want to say. Then, as you're able, add detail under those big ideas. Answer questions like: Who cares? So what? Why does this matter? Don't worry about how the words sound—the text of the outline is for you, not your readers.

After you've gotten your rough outline together, look for opportunities to group and collapse related ideas. Where are you repeating yourself? Where might you need to add a larger point to tie a few of the smaller ones together? Give a thought to the order of things, too. What information will be most useful to have toward the top of the copy? What can wait until the end?

Clear thinking is powerful. With a strong outline, some of your writing will seem to write itself!

New version announcement post

- Headline (simple and clear) [70 characters max]
    - announcing a new version of the app...
- Sub-head [150 characters max]
    - all new design, several great new features
- Introduction
    - a new version of the app is coming
    - it will be a paid upgrade
    - we're excited about it and hope you are too
- Body (headers + 1-3 paragraphs each)
    - Announcing the new version
        - It's true, we're finally releasing 3.0
        - We're most excited for: [something]
    - What's in the new version
        - now uses native cloud sync
            - will still work w/ Dropbox or G Drive
        - completely fresh design
        - imports old projects seamlessly
        - (link to full feature breakdown on product page)
    - What happens to the old version
        - nothing will change if you don't want it to
        - can upgrade and run both side-by-side
        - honoring all current support agreements
- Wrap-up
    - Call out and link to developer blog
    - See a preview here [product page]
- Promo area (inset)
    - Sign up to be notified
    - Email capture

FIG 1.3: An outline reflects both the shape of your ideas and the shape of your interface. In this example, the top level of the outline is used to mark out different sections of content within the post.

Templates

Templates are any tool that says "Structure your writing in this particular way." Content strategists have all kinds of names for the templates they make: page tables, page description diagrams, content templates, and more. Templates are sometimes built into content management systems or headless content systems like Gather Content.

Templates can generally be understood as a two-column table (**FIG 1.4**). The left column defines what needs to be written (including constraints like word or character limits), and the right column provides space to write the thing. You can turn any design that needs words into a template by simply listing the various design elements down the left column.

As the name implies, templates are a great choice when you have to make the same sort of thing more than once.

Meta Info

Browser Title *(visible in address bar and search results)*	
URL Slug *(trailing end of page URL)*	
External search description *(reader-friendly description of page content for search results previews)*	
Social share description(s)	
Internal search description	

Product Header Area

Product full name *Include required ® or ™ or other marks.*	
Product URL	
Support URL	
Plain-language description *Not a slogan or tagline. Write a meaningful, clear, one sentence description for a general audience. No links.* ***200 characters.***	
Positioning headline *Key message in headline format.* ***200 characters.***	
Features/Body *One to three paragraphs. Links okay. Bullets okay if bookended by paragraph text.* ***800 characters.***	
PDF brochure URL *Optional*	
Marketing video URL *Optional*	

FIG 1.4: A template with descriptions of what's needed on the left, and room for copy on the right, allows you to "fill in" your writing assignment as you go. It's easily extendable with additional columns to add things like approvals, translations, metadata, and more.

Inventories

Inventories work well when you have lots of little bits of texts, as with interface copy. Inventories are made in spreadsheets, where it's easy to keep track of all those little bits and their associated data.

You can start by sequentially numbering text elements in a wireframe—this creates a quick inventory that connects what's been designed and what's being written (**FIG 1.5**).

The resulting identification system makes it easier to manage your work and collaborate on it with others. Having all of your strings ID'd makes them "talkable"—the difference between:

ID	Element Type	Description	Text	Notes
2.x	screen	sign-up screen	n/a	
2.0	headline	form header	Create Your Account	
username				
2.1	label	username entry	Username:	
2.1.1	field placeholder	username entry	Be friendly! Other users will see this.	
2.1.2a	validation error	too short	Usernames must be at least 5 characters.	
2.1.2b	validation error	special characters	Usernames can only include letters and numbers.	
2.1.2c	validation error	restricted	Sorry, that name is not available.	e.g. admin, AwesomeCo
password				
2.2	label	password entry	Choose a password:	
2.2.1	field placeholder	password entry	At least 8 characters.	
2.2.2a	validation error	password too short	Too short!	
2.2.2b	validation error	banned list	Try something more complicated.	e.g. password, 12345678
2.2.2b	validation error	invalid password message	Sorry, that's not working.	
zip				
2.3	label	zip code	Your ZIP:	
2.3.1	field placeholder	zip code	e.g. 90210	(not validated/required)
2.7	text	existing account sign in	Already have an account? [Sign in.]	link second sentence
2.8	button	continue button	Create Account	grayed out until username + password validate
2.9	return key	keyboard form submit	Continue	UIReturnKeyType

FIG 1.5: A spreadsheet inventory helps you track every string you need for an interface, and gives you room to capture all of the error states and alternative messages that might not fit neatly into a high-fidelity design mockup.

"Do you have the approved copy for G 7.1?"

and:

"Do you have the approved copy for the text that goes under the button on the fifth screen of the third section of the app? No, not that button, the other button. Right. Wait, that doesn't fit, what version are you looking at?"

MAKE SPACE TO WRITE

We're almost to the writing part of writing! To create your draft copy, you'll need three things: a place to put the words, a place to put yourself, and some time to do the writing.

Prepare your digital space

Thanks to our friends Copy and Paste, you can usually do your writing in one environment and move it to another without too much fuss. You don't have to do all of your writing in Microsoft Word or the CMS just because that's where it needs to end up.

You want a writing environment that thinks about writing the way that you do. It should make it easy for you to write quickly. It should make it easy for you to collaborate with others and complete editing and review steps in your workflow. And it should be appropriate to the type of content you're working on—a word processor focused on desktop publishing might well be overkill for writing out a few strings for your interface.

Web-based writing environments can be fantastic, and offer advantages when it comes to version control and collaboration. Be cautious about doing your work in a web browser, however. There are many points of potential failure: web browser crashes, service outages, accidental refreshes—you get the idea. (I don't think I'll ever break the habit of mashing ⌘S after finishing a paragraph.)

Consider a workflow where the bulk of your composing—those big sprints of "doing the writing"—happens in a stable local application on your computer. You can then copy your work into whatever web-based tool you need to use for editing. We'll talk about this more with version management in Chapter 3.

Your design environment might work well as a writing environment. If you go that route, create a duplicate version of your project before you start, so you've got the freedom to be a bit messy. Once you've got some final, authoritative text, you can drop it back into the master file in place of those squiggly lines.

Prepare your physical space

I once worked in a small, open-plan office at a startup company. Our designer, Amanda, took to wearing her "design hoodie" on days when she had to get a lot of work done. When the hood was up, we weren't allowed to bother her for any reason. No "quick questions." No "Have you seen that video where..." Hood up = DESIGN TIME, no interruptions.

Whether it's a hoodie or an office with a door or a coffee shop where no one knows you, it helps to do the writing in a space where you won't be interrupted. Developers and designers know that there are some kinds of work that require you to build a bit of intellectual momentum, and that being interrupted, even briefly, can kill that momentum. Writing is that kind of work, too.

This is challenging in some office cultures. Strive for it anyway. Try talking to your supervisor or project managers about ways to carve out the time and space you need to write. If writing is an infrequent responsibility and you have a lot of demands on your time, you may end up needing to shift your schedule a bit. Try writing early in the morning or late in the day when other folks are less likely to use your ears as an inbox.

Oh, and in case it needs saying: when it's time to write, turn off notifications on as many things as you can get away with. If closing your email client or shutting off your phone gives you anxiety, try a timer—the world's not going to end if you're offline for fifteen minutes. And if it does, look on the bright side: no more deadlines!

Clear (some of) your calendar

"Hey Siri, add appointment to write all the things from 1 p.m. to 3 p.m. tomorrow."

Blocking off time on your calendar to write—and protecting that time against meetings and interruptions—is a good start, and more than many writers are able to pull off. So do it if you can.

But be honest with yourself about that time. Two hours on the calendar rarely equals two nonstop hours of writing. (If you figure out how to do that, please tell me.)

Timeboxing can help you make the most of your writing time. Make a quick list of what you want to work on in a given period, and apportion each item some of that time. You could do this per screen or page (e.g., landing page, thirty minutes), by content type (e.g., confirmation buttons, twenty minutes), by user journey (e.g., password reset flow, thirty minutes), or whatever else makes sense for your brain and your assignment.

FIRST DRAFT INBOUND

Preparation isn't the part of writing that people tend to think of as writing, but it's no less important. Having a clear assignment, lots of inputs and ideas to work with, and a sense of how the rest of your work is going to go sets you up for a more efficient process and successful writing outcomes.

For the marketing copy on a new, large website, you might spend weeks in the Prepare phase. For the interface language on a single app screen, twenty or thirty minutes of preparation might be enough. A little planning up front goes a long way.

Take a breather if you need to, and get ready for the phase with all of the typing and crying: Compose.

2

COMPOSE

IT'S TIME TO COMPOSE YOURSELF! Err, your draft, that is.

The work you'll do in this phase is what most people refer to when they talk about writing—never mind all that pesky planning and editing work, right?

I told you earlier that writing isn't magic, but that doesn't mean we can't use a few tricks to make it easier. Those tricks revolve around two objectives: to write quickly and to write everything.

WRITE QUICKLY

I want you to write quickly, for two reasons:

1. If you try to compose the perfect draft one perfect word at a time, you'll never get the writing done.
2. Good clear writing comes from good clear thinking. The less time your thoughts have to rattle around in your head, the more time they can spend in the clear light of day—and the better they'll sound in your design.

Do a rough-in

One way to write quickly is to do as little writing as possible. Start with a *rough-in*: grab all of the relevant text from your inputs, and put it on or near where it needs to go in your design (**FIG 2.1**).

If there's one slot for a user testimonial, for instance, and you have a few to choose from, grab several that might work and drop them into that box. If you need to write labels for a tabbed navigation element, go ahead and drop in the simplest and most obvious label for each. A navigation bar that reads "Home | user stuff | promo stuff | settings and options" has you a lot further along already than "Label | label | label | label."

The sooner you move away from squiggly lines and *lorem ipsum*, the sooner you can get the writing done. A good rough-in lets you skip right past blank-page paralysis to *re*-writing, which goes a lot faster.

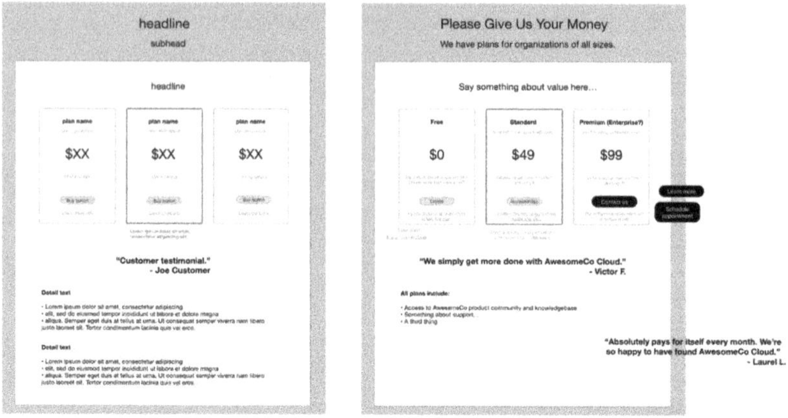

FIG 2.1: While both of these are unfinished, the wireframe on the right, with roughed-in copy, gives a much better idea of what the page is about—and what still needs to be written.

Use a scratchpad

If you had to suffer through standardized tests, you might already be familiar with paper scratchpads. A *scratchpad* is anything that helps you separate THE THING (i.e. your working draft) from NOT THE THING (everything else).

A digital scratchpad helps you write quickly because you're never stuck staring at a blinking cursor. You can jot out a mini outline in the scratchpad, or move text that's not working into the scratchpad and try again. I'll often cut and paste the text from my rough-in over to the scratchpad as I go, then refer to it while I'm writing true draft copy.

Scratchpads can also provide minor version control. Since I cut and paste sentences from my draft to my scratchpad instead of deleting them completely, I'm less likely to accidentally lose something. Having alternative text tucked away in your scratchpad can also help if the first review of your work doesn't go so great.

Don't forget that you're allowed to use actual paper, too. It's amazing how helpful it can be to jot a few words down on paper when you're having trouble maintaining momentum with your keyboard.

Skip the details

The things we need to write often include facts, figures, and statistics that we don't have readily at hand. And sometimes we run up against something that doesn't exist yet, like a link that hasn't been created or a product that hasn't been named.

In these situations, it's okay—preferable, even—to use a placeholder. Drop something in that will call attention to itself later and keep writing. DO NOT OPEN WIKIPEDIA. DO NOT POST IN SLACK. DO NOT ASK SIRI. Just keep writing.

Journalists use "TK" as a placeholder, which means "to come"—the unusual letter combination makes it easy to find-and-replace later. I myself use NARF, Pinky's catchphrase—yes, as in *Pinky and the Brain*—for the same reason. I also do a lot of ad hoc marking of things to follow up on, like // fix this later // or [NARF add link here].

If your writing environment is also a design environment, you might want to set off placeholders in another color or style. Whatever you do, pick something that's hard to miss during editing—just do it quickly and keep writing.

Reduce friction

Try to notice what causes frustration, slowdowns, or distractions while you're writing. A small irritation in your writing boots can add up to a hike-ending blister after an hour or two on the composing trail.

If you find yourself fussing with fonts and formatting before all the words are written, consider writing in a low-fidelity environment like a text editor.

If your writing environment's guidance (like automatic spelling correction, capitalization, lists, and styling) are getting in your way, turn 'em off! These little demons can make composing a draft feel like a game of Whac-A-Mole. There's a time and a place to check your spelling, style your quotes, and indent lists properly, and it's not now.

Finally, I recommend adopting a "lazy" mentality and occasionally asking yourself if there's a faster or automated way to do what you're about to do. Do you need to write this feature description from scratch, or can you borrow one from elsewhere in the app? Do you need to type that obnoxious CamelCase™ product name every time, or can you create a keyboard shortcut to format it automatically?

WRITE EVERYTHING

If you're still lost on how to start or what to write, you may need to revisit your inputs and assignment. But more than likely, at this point, you just need to start writing.

Pick something easy to get your fingers moving. (You don't have to start at the beginning.) Continue writing, and get the whole thing written before you start perfecting individual parts of it. Editing comes later, and besides, what you write in one area might impact what you write in another area.

You may want to track your progress against your outline, template, or inventory by crossing things out or changing colors after you've got something covered.

Write one thing at a time

The best way to write also generates the best kind of writing: say just one thing at a time. Say one thing in your headings. Say one thing on your buttons. Say one thing in the tooltip text, one thing in the error message, one thing in each paragraph.

Writers get stuck (and readers get lost) when the words are trying to express too much at once. Words are powerful, yes, but still bound by pesky constraints like "time" and "how brains work."

If you're feeling overwhelmed, or the words are coming slowly, narrow your scope. Focus in and say just one thing.

Practice your ACBs

The ACBs are a set of writing and editing lenses created by Ken Rand in his book *The 10% Solution*. The acronym stands for Accuracy, Clarity, and Brevity. The order of the lenses is as important as the lenses themselves.

Accuracy

Start by writing something that is objectively true. The labels in our interface copy need to correspond with what actually happens when the user interacts with those elements. The features and benefits in our marketing copy need to reflect the actual product the user is signing up for, not an imagined or ideal version. The product copy needs to provide real, useful guidance. If what we're writing is wrong, we're already sunk.

Accuracy in interface copy requires understanding how the interface actually behaves. If you're not sure, ask! You might be surprised how often you'll discover a button, link, or other element whose behavior is a mystery, even if you designed it. Find the answer, design the answer, or carve those unknowns out of the scope of your current assignment (and be sure to flag them for follow-up). A simple example: don't write DELETE (the file from the system) when you really mean REMOVE (the file from the list).

Accuracy in product copy often depends on understanding your reader's context. Something that's true for users that are signed in, for instance, might not be true for users that aren't. For your first draft, write out what you think is true to the best of your understanding, and flag anything that you think might need more attention.

Accuracy in marketing copy can be trickier. Stakeholders are often pushing for superlatives—the latest, greatest, best, most amazing. But accuracy isn't just about the truth; it's also a way to cut through the fluff and express more powerful and compelling ideas. For example, let's say you're editing a list of features for a new product and come across this:

Secure storage means you'll never have to worry about someone else accessing your important files.

Not bad, but let's apply our accuracy lens and see what happens. We might ask: "Is it true that users will *never* have to worry about this? It is true that it's secure? What does *secure* mean? Is it true that no one else will *ever* access the files? Does that include our support department?"

Statements that *feel* accurate to your product and marketing teams aren't always objective statements of truth. What's secure to one person might be risky to another, and your product can't control what people will or won't worry about.

So let's say you look back at your inputs, and it turns out that your company uses an industry-leading encryption protocol, enables two-factor authentication by default, and has undergone a vigorous auditing process conducted by a well-respected outside agency. Nice! So instead of the (not objectively true) marketing text, you might write:

The most secure file storage solution our industry has ever seen.

And that could be punched up even more with links to information about your security practices and so on. A big change and a powerful improvement, all from one little question: Is this true?

Clarity

After you have your facts straight, you want to focus on making your writing clear—that is, straightforward, simple, and easy to understand.

To create clarity, look for opportunities to:

- replace resplendently fantastical fancy language with simpler language (and uncommon words with common ones)
- put things in a logical order
- add supporting information
- add examples and anecdotes to reinforce your point

- delete things that don't support your main idea
- define concepts that users might be unfamiliar with

Context is also an important part of clarity. Take a fresh look at the context-creating inputs from your Prepare phase to make sure that the text you've prepared will be readily understood by your audience.

Sometimes the easiest way to bring clarity to your writing is to simply rewrite it. Unlike in real life, where whatever stupid thing that just came out of your mouth at the party can never be unsaid, writing allows for instant do-overs. You don't owe anything to your first draft (except accuracy, of course).

(Rewrites are a balancing act. You want to keep writing, and write quickly, yes. And you want to leave the bulk of your editing work for the next phase. But in practice, doing the writing tends to involve quick iterative cycles of writing something and then revising what you've just written.)

Clarity is in the middle of this ACB sandwich because text can never be clear if it's not accurate or too brief.

Brevity

Brevity is last—it's admirable, but it should never cause you to sacrifice accuracy or clarity. *Short* doesn't automatically mean easier to read or understand.

When I was a UX writer on a design team, I consulted daily with designers who were stuck because they *started* with brevity. Sometimes they were trying to write text directly within the confines of a wireframe (and without accurate character constraints). Other times, a well-intentioned but ill-informed stakeholder was pushing them to "make it shorter," because that's the only advice they knew about writing for the web.

"How do I make it fit?" is the right question at the wrong time. Start by writing out a complete idea, *then* refine and trim. For instance, you might start with:

> *Click this button to submit the information in the form and also join our mailing list.*

That's obviously quite lengthy and not good. But it's written! And it's something to work from, as opposed to the nothing you had before. Another quick pass—focusing on the verbs—might get you down to:

Submit and Join

That's more concise, but also sounds like the slogan of a sci-fi totalitarian regime. But it has the key information, and gives you a foundation for further revision.

Laying out messages like that for an entire screen or flow puts the whole story in front of you—which makes what you need to say, and where, much more apparent. For instance, after writing just that little bit, you might realize that submitting the form and joining the mailing list should be separate options, requiring a checkbox and message below the button. Mark it for discussion and move on to the next bit of writing—there's no reason to perfect the text of a button that might change.

KEEP WRITING

If this were a longer book, I could muddle your mind with all kinds of additional tips and tricks and hacks and methods for "doing" the writing. But it might be for the best that this isn't a longer book. No matter how many tricks you employ, the only thing that really gets that first draft done is you making the clickity-clackity sound on your keyboard.

Write quickly, with tools that make writing easier, in an environment conducive to getting the writing done. Repeat this until you've written a decent, complete draft that meets the requirements of your assignment.

Drafts can be rough. They might be messy. But some of it, hopefully, is good and smart—maybe even brilliant. But the draft is just the start. Next? We Edit.

3

EDIT

THERE'S A BIT OF A FUZZY LINE between composing and editing. Often, to reach that complete first draft, we'll cut and paste words and phrases, rewrite ideas, maybe even scratch a whole screen's worth of text and start over.

This is inevitable, though perhaps not ideal. "Tweaking" the text while we write will catch errors and improve phrasing, but it won't elevate the consistency, clarity, and quality of the writing.

For our purposes, *editing* is about substantively improving the writing. Don't confuse this with proofreading, where you fix typos and punctuation. That stuff is important, too, but comes at the end of the process, which is why we'll talk more about it in the next chapter.

The mental shift from writing to editing doesn't happen automatically. If you've just finished your first big run through the Compose phase, job one is to take a break. Not too long, mind you. A lunch break will do. A walk around the block. A hoverboard trip to the all-you-can-eat activated yogurt buffet, if you work in one of those futuristic Silicon Valley offices.

Going somewhere, changing your workspace, or otherwise physically marking a shift in mindset allows you to sit down to your work with a fresh intention. This helps you focus on what you're doing right now: editing, editing, editing.

And hands off that Delete key! There's something important we need to cover first: ch-ch-ch-ch-changes.

TRACK YOUR CHANGES

Moving from composing text to editing text means that you'll have *versions*. There's the first version, and then the version after you correct that obvious spelling mistake, and the version after you rewrite the headline, and so on. Every change creates a new version of the text. Add collaborators and other editors to the mix, and suddenly there are versions of your versions. And versions of those versions!

You need an anchor in this version storm: a system to track and manage revisions before you begin editing. Whether you're revising a single error message string inside a web app, or trying to put some polish on a thirty-page white paper, the principles are the same:

- You want to preserve your first draft for reference.
- You want to be able to undo (and redo) changes that you and others make to the text with relative ease.
- You want to keep track of the who and the why of any changes more seriously than correcting typos and spelling errors.

Editing can be dangerous. Move too quickly, and you can lose the thread of what you were trying to accomplish—or lose good work altogether. It's like a big gust of wind blowing loose papers off an old-timey novelist's desk straight into the fireplace, except in this case you're the wind *and* the fire. (The paper was your chance at leaving early today.)

Tracking this stuff is especially important if you're doing lots of fast loops (say, in Agile-ish environments) where sign-offs happen incrementally. You don't want your text to surprise anyone the next time they look at it. And if they *are* surprised, you'll want to be able to explain and defend your choices.

There are as many methods of managing versions as there are teams and workflows. Let's look at a few of the more common ones.

Haxonomies

Haxonomy is a fancy name for a simple thing you're probably already doing somewhere. The name is a portmanteau of *hack* and *taxonomy*. A taxonomy, in the general sense, is a method of classification. When the type of organization you want isn't available where you want it, you can "hack" it in. Hence: haxonomy.

Many people instinctively manage document versions with haxonomies in the file name. This leads to names like:

> *2018-02-28 Big Deliverable Version 5 FINAL copy ACTUAL FINAL—SK + KH Edits.docx.PDF*

Instead, plan your haxonomies. Some useful file-naming patterns include:

- An incremental number system (like V1, V2, V3, etc.), updated each time *before* you make any substantive changes to the text—the biggest number will always be the most recent version.
- Initials to indicate whose edits the version contains (e.g., Book Draft—SK).
- Shorthand for process steps that have been completed, such as "LGL" for a version of the text that the lawyers have already signed off on.

Where you store files can communicate information, too—for instance, making the canonical version of the text the only file allowed in a particular shared folder.

It's best not to improvise these things. Without a clear plan, shared by the whole team, things like color codes and tags and folders will turn into a noisy mess.

Changelogs

Changelogs are just what they sound like: a written log of changes that have been published or otherwise incorporated into the thing that's been changed.

Changelogs are a concept you can use on any project, no fancy software required. You could even keep one right at the top of the document itself. Having the history of the writing paired closely *with* the writing makes it easier for everyone to understand how the text ended up the way that it did.

This is especially handy during reviews with persnickety stakeholders who try to poke holes in your process:

Stakeholder: "Where is this writing coming from? Has marketing looked at this?"
You (so on top of version management): "Why, yes, you can see that on June 19, we had a collaborative working session on the text with marketing."
Stakeholder: "Hmm. Well. Okay, good."

Make notes about what you change as you change it, and include dates. This is tedious, yes, but gets less so over time as you build the habit and get used to the benefits.

Here are some example entries you might put in a manual changelog:

- *02/13 DN—Wrote first draft based on outline from support team*
- *02/17 MJM—Revised all CTA strings based on style guide (incl. title case on buttons)*
- *2/18 DN—Completely new intro copy dropped at VP's request*
- *2/25 (PM update email)—Reviewed by support (Maurice) for accuracy, gave okay*

You may think you'll remember these types of things, but you won't. Pairing your changelog with a basic versioning system will make it *much* easier to navigate all of the forthcoming trickiness of getting text reviewed and approved.

Automatic version control

Online environments like Google Documents and features like Track Changes in Microsoft Word do a decent job of highlighting what's different since the last time you looked at the text, but they can't read your mind. If the editing process takes you through several deeply different versions of the text—different conceptual approaches, a different tone, a different structure—it can be hard to return to a specific, earlier approach.

Don't rely exclusively on autosaves and cloud backups—documenting decisions and intent are as much a part of smart version control as monitoring changes to the text itself.

If you work with code, you might already be a version control pro with a tool like GitHub. These types of systems are great for knowing exactly what changed and when, but the "why" is still up to you: be sure to comment on those commits.

KNOW WHY YOU'RE EDITING

Editing requires an intention, a lens of sorts—an answer to the question "Editing for what?" You could rewrite a draft fifty times, but if you don't have a goal in mind during those rewrites, how can you know whether it's getting any better? Having a lens changes your mindset from merely *reading* the text to *evaluating* the text against particular criteria. Let's look at a few of the more common editing lenses.

Focus

Editing to make your writing more focused means cutting out stuff that isn't related to the key goals and messages of your design. Writing is focused when every word—*every* word—is serving a clear purpose.

When you edit for focus, you might start by skimming through the text and marking any words that seem incidental, frivolous, trivial, or disconnected. Ask yourself what, if anything, they're contributing to the writing. If you don't have a good answer, cut it.

Editing for focus can also mean evaluating your text against your stated goals. How well does it articulate the key messages? If the goal is to sell, is it compelling and persuasive? If the goal is to educate, is it clear and complete? Does it anticipate and answer key questions?

Simplicity

Everyone will tell you that simplicity is a good thing. But how do you actually achieve it? If you feel like the writing is too complex and could benefit from being simpler, there are three key levers you can manipulate:

- **Structure:** How it's organized. Things that feel complex often feel simpler once they're in the right order. It's the same information, mostly the same words, but organized in a way that adds context and clarifies the meaning.

- **Language:** The words you use. Many organizations strive to apply principles of plain language to their writing—using the simplest words possible in any given situation. Plain language doesn't mean dumbed-down or boring; directness and clarity make room for your big ideas to pop.
- **Concept:** The big idea behind the writing. Clear concepts keep things simple. If you're explaining something new or complex, consider a metaphor that's relatable for your primary audience.

Readability

Is the writing easy or hard to read? Is it easy or hard to understand? Can people follow along, or will they get lost?

Readability isn't about *legibility* in the design sense, but about what's happening in a reader's head as they process the words.

If we want our writing to be readable and user-friendly, we need to do more work now so that our readers have less work to do later. For instance:

- Extract the most important point and put it right at the top.
- Clearly specify the next action the reader needs to take.
- State whom the information is for (or not for).
- Vary the lengths of sentences and paragraphs. (Rhythmic variety is easier to read.)

Readability tests can help evaluate your text based on things like overall length and the number of syllables in your words. While not a foolproof metric, it's useful for comparing newer versions of text with older ones to see if you're headed in the right direction. You could also benchmark against similar text within your design, or within a competitor's design. For some recommended readability tools, see the Resources section.

Consistency

Editing for consistency means making sure your writing agrees with itself, and that it agrees with all of the other stuff it's connected to. Little inconsistencies creep in everywhere: here it's the "welcome" screen, there it's the "sign-in" screen. Here it's a "free trial," there it's a "test drive." The button on this contact form says "Submit," but that one says "Send."

Part of your job is to ensure that the words you use to describe product features and interface components are consistent throughout the experience. One way to achieve this is through the application of a *controlled vocabulary*.

Controlled vocabularies are like custom dictionaries. They can exist as a simple list of terms and definitions; you could even incorporate them as a layer in a design pattern library.

Editing for consistency is fairly straightforward, provided you have controlled vocabulary documentation or an interface element inventory. Use the search function within your writing environment to find the listed terms—or the terms the list is meant to replace.

Strength

Do the words make an impact? Does the writing feel strong, or does it feel passive? Passive voice is almost guaranteed to suck the strength out of your writing.

To eliminate passive voice, you first have to recognize it. Talking about subjects and objects and diagramming sentences is boring, so let's say: passive voice has no ownership—it feels weak—whereas active voice takes a stand—it feels strong.

Compare, for instance:

- **Passive voice:** "Mistakes were made."
- **Active voice:** "I screwed up. My bad."

In the passive example, no one is *doing* anything. It's weak. Who made the mistakes? No one, apparently. Passive voice isn't wrong, per se, but it has less impact than active voice. In active voice, there's *action*, not just *existence*.

Putting your ideas in the right order also adds impact and strength. In a first draft, you're figuring out what to write as you're writing it, which means that the most interesting idea—the one with the most impact—often ends up at the end of your sentence, paragraph, or flow. Move it to the top, and *boom*! Writing so strong, it's flexing for selfies.

Tone

Getting the right tone for your writing means that it's emotionally appropriate to the audience and subject matter. It's about finding the right "vibe," the right "level" for the writing.

With a clear assignment to guide you (meaning you know the audience and context for your writing), odds are good that your tone is already fairly appropriate. Still, tone can be a useful editing lens on a screen-by-screen or paragraph-by-paragraph basis. Just like in real life, one inappropriate comment at the wrong moment can throw off an entire experience.

There are a few specific angles on tone that often apply to business and design writing. Let's take a closer look.

Urgency

Buy now! Ends soon! Subscribe in the next thirty seconds or there will never be rainbows again!

Creating a sense of urgency can be useful, but, when done poorly, risks ringing hollow and making users skeptical. It can even do long-term damage to whether or not users trust you and your brand. Urgency must be applied appropriately.

Not appropriate:

> *URGENT! ATTENTION REQUIRED! We value your feedback. If you do not respond to our previous survey in the next 3 days, you will LOSE your ability to be entered into a contest with 8 million other customers to win a single $25 Outback Steakhouse Gift Certificate.*

Better:

> *URGENT! ATTENTION REQUIRED! Your domain will expire in 3 days. It is NOT set to renew. If you do not manually renew, you could lose access to your domain name forever.*

Be thoughtful about your writing's necessary level of urgency. Sometimes the right thing to do is to slow people down. Sometimes the right thing to do *is* to freak them out (just a little). Get clear on what's appropriate for your design, and edit accordingly.

Scale

Editing for appropriate scale means asking yourself how important the subject really is, and communicating that importance accurately and effectively.

Hyperbole is a crutch. Calling everything the *biggest, best, greatest,* and *most fantastic ever* is the sign of a weak mind. A weak, orange, treasonous mind.

Not every product update is revolutionary. Not every feature is groundbreaking. Are you expressing a big idea or a small idea? Does everyone *need* to stop in their tracks and pay attention to this, or is it okay if it only reaches some users?

Emotion

The emotional aspect of your writing needs to be appropriate to the subject matter. Delight and humor can be wonderful things, but they shouldn't be shoved into every experience. It's perfectly fine for some experiences—and the writing that supports them—to be serious, clear, or even somber.

Timing is a critical factor in conveying the appropriate emotion with your writing. For instance, users don't want cutesy messages while their mortgage payment is being processed.

The earlier prep work you've done to understand your audience and the context of the design writing will go a long way toward helping you convey the appropriate emotional tone with your words. It may be worth revisiting that information ahead of an editing pass to put you in an audience-focused state of mind.

DO THE EDITING

At this point, you might be asking: how exactly do I *do* the editing?

To effectively edit your writing, you need to introduce a layer of abstraction between you and the copy. (If you've ever flipped text in a design upside-down to check the kerning, you know what I'm talking about.)

That abstraction layer can be a hack, a tool, or another person (like an editor)—whatever you need to approach the work with more distance and objectivity.

Choose editing tools that make you look closely and carefully at the actual words that have been written, not just your impression of what it *says*. These are a few methods that work reliably, no matter what you've written.

Read it

At the risk of stating the obvious: it's a good idea to read what you've written before you show it to someone else. This readback will help you catch major errors like unfinished sentences and big copy-and-paste goofs.

The problem with reading, however, is that you're very good at it. Too good! You've been reading your whole life, and as with anything you've practiced that much, a lot of it happens on autopilot. Your pattern-optimized brain (thanks, evolution!) wants to make sense of whatever mess of letters it encounters, and it will lie, cheat, and steal to make that happen.

That means that a quiet, in-your-head readback is not a great way to catch some of the more pernicious errors of grammar, spelling, and formatting that will plague your copy. There are smarter approaches to reading your work that will help you edit. Let's look at a few.

Read it out loud

Reading your text out loud (into the air, making actual sounds with your mouth) is one of the most recommended bits of editing advice for writers.

However, I know from experience that if I simply tell you to read it out loud, you'll think to yourself, "Oh, yes, that is very good advice. I will read my writing out loud from now on." But then you won't actually do it. You're not going to do it!

Why don't people do it? Lots of reasons, I suppose. It takes too long? It feels silly? You work in an open-plan office (a.k.a. Writer's Hell) and it would bug your coworkers?

Still, if it's a very important piece, *do* try hard to read it out loud at a normal speaking pace. You can print your text and take it on a walk (don't forget a red pen!). Or slip into an unused conference room. I sometimes read my text "out loud" to myself at a very low volume.

While you're reading, listen. Listen for anywhere that you trip up, anything that sounds funny, anything that's hard to say, anywhere that you got lost. Mark those passages and consider them for revision.

Read it out loud to a person

This is especially good for marketing copy. Remember, real human people are going to have to read what you write. If you can't read it out loud to someone without feeling completely awkward, that's pretty telling.

There's also something magical about "performing" your text for someone—it engages a very different part of the brain. You may well surprise yourself with a creative improvisation as you're speaking the words that wouldn't have occurred to you as you were writing them.

(And yes, you can totally read it to your dog. That has the added benefit of being *adorable*.)

Have the computer read it to you

Text-to-speech is a wonderful accessibility tool, and just so happens to be handy for writers, too. I frequently make my Mac read things back to me. In many apps, you can highlight the text you want read and select a read-aloud option, and the computer will read absolutely everything in the most literal way. This is great for catching repeated words and other typos that your brain might trick you into thinking aren't there.

Have a person read it to you

Having someone else read it out loud makes the feedback very direct. Readers who are not you might put the emphasis in unexpected places, revealing potential ambiguities. You can hear where they hesitate and where they speed up. You don't even have to ask them for their thoughts (though you might as well)—just hearing them read it will reveal plenty.

Ask for feedback

Stakeholder reviews—for both design and writing—are often built into our processes. What doesn't occur to many writers, however, is that they may be able to ask stakeholders for *feedback* before asking them for *approval*.

This may be a new idea for your stakeholders, too, and thus needs to be approached carefully. How you frame your invitation matters. Dropping a meeting invite on someone's calendar called "Review onboarding text" sets a very different tone than sending a message asking if you can borrow a few minutes of their time at the end of the day to run some preliminary approaches by them.

Be clear what kind of feedback you're looking for, and ask specific questions. For example:

- *Does this include all of the information we need to communicate to customers?*
- *We're trying out a lighthearted tone. How would you feel if the final draft ends up sounding something like this?*
- *I'm focusing on structure right now. Is this the right order to tell this story?*
- *I want to know what questions you think customers will have after reading this.*

It helps to articulate for stakeholders where you are in the process, and to assure them that, yes, they'll have a chance to see the final text, yes, it's going to go through legal, yes, someone is going to proofread it, yes, they can see it before it goes live on the website, etc.

While careful framing helps, it won't work for everyone. You may simply have to grin and bear it while they circle typos and missing ™ symbols. Other stakeholders will insist on seeing the writing in the design, or in the browser, or on paper—consider which delivery method will solicit useful feedback from the stakeholder in question. (And you'll eventually learn that some people just can't help you, no matter how you frame it.)

If you make changes based on the feedback, or just get unstuck, be sure to note that in your changelog, and let your collaborator know that they contributed. (Never assume that a stakeholder will remember what they told you when it comes time to approve the final text. Keep your receipts!)

Collaborate with others

Sometimes, for whatever reason, you just can't quite figure out how to say what you're trying to say. Or you've said it, and it's blah. Time to bring in a fresh pair of eyes.

Collaborating with colleagues can be one of the quickest and most effective ways to help you get unstuck—or to unsuck a particularly rough passage. Even brief conversations can yield big outcomes.

A handy framing device for these collaborations is to ask, "How would you approach this?" That's more freeing than "What's the best way to write this?" and more forward-looking than "What's wrong with this?"

Build a buddy system with other writers so you can bounce text off of each other regularly. Fellow designers can be collaborators, too—they can help you tease out whether you're looking at a design problem, a writing problem, a product problem, or something else entirely. Running your drafts past coworkers also creates opportunities to learn from each other and to increase consistency in language and terminology.

LOCK IT IN

Sometimes, the hardest part about editing is stopping. It can feel like there's always more to improve upon, more people you should run the copy by, more of the word count you should trim away.

This is part of why we plan our writing workflow—editing rarely feels "done," but if we've completed our workflow steps, it's done *enough*. Eventually, you have to say: "This is the text. These are the words. We are moving forward with these words."

You might not be there yet, and that's okay. If editing helped you identify some gaps, you might need to move back to composing. If the text still feels really rough, you might need to add additional editing steps, or find a friend to help. And if it's all a big mess, you might need to re-evaluate your assignment and prepare a fresh plan to get the writing done.

Eventually, though, you'll be able to lock in your draft. If your writing assignment were a term paper, at this point you'd be able to hit Send (and then hit the bar...or the gym, or the beach, or the slopes, I don't know your jam.). But in the world of design writing, we're not done yet. To get the writing really and truly done, you have to Finish.

4

FINISH

WRITING IN A DESIGN CONTEXT can feel like stepping in quicksand—not *real* quicksand, but 1980s cinematic quicksand that swallows children whole in seconds. Luckily, you've already got a trusty whip—or vine, or long docile snake...whatever your preferred method of quicksand escape may be. That whip is the assignment.

Clearly articulating the assignment, as we did in the Prepare phase, lets you know when you can finally put your pencil down and step away from the role of writer, *even and especially if the design itself is not yet done.*

This last phase, Finish, includes all of the steps big and small you need to take care of to complete your writing assignment, including approvals, hand-offs, reintegrating it into the design, and reflecting on your work.

GETTING THE WRITING APPROVED

Most of the things we write for a design project will be subject to review and approval by someone else—a design lead, a product owner, a business stakeholder. Whether the text is reviewed and approved together with the full design, or separately, or some combination thereof, will depend on your design project and organizational culture.

It's hard to get anyone to pay attention to anything, let alone to get busy stakeholders to slow down and *read* something, carefully and critically. Like anything else you design, part of your job is to sell and present your work. Luckily, all of the skills you have for presenting design work apply to presenting your writing.

If you're bringing writing for review for the first time, try to find a coworker who's already gone through the process, and ask their advice. Ask about any quirks or preferences of the people who will be doing the reviewing, and how they give feedback. Some stakeholders need a little translation. I worked at a place once where hearing the CEO say "I don't completely hate this" was cause for celebration, and a profanity-laden tirade often just meant "This needs a bit more work." Colorful guy!

You will want to anticipate stakeholder questions, prepare answers to those questions, and present those answers in a sensible order before they have a chance to ask them. And I do mean *present*—you will be best served by holding a meeting and walking people through this information, rather than firing off a draft over email and hoping for the best.

As the writer, there are some things you'll want to be prepared for during these final approvals. They will probably be familiar from your experience as a designer:

- **The swoop and poop:** Just what it sounds like—somebody swoops in and takes a shit all over everything you've written. A clear assignment and a well-maintained changelog can help serve as your shit umbrella, since sometimes the pooping is motivated by a mistaken belief that everything about the writing is arbitrary. Identifying important stakeholders early and integrating them into your process can help alleviate this; people are less likely to shit on something if they feel like they were part of making it.
- **Goalpost shifting:** You wrote the text to accomplish X, and yet someone is complaining that it doesn't do Y. They're evaluating your writing against a different (or more ambitious) goal. It could be that the project's goals have changed; it could also be that they are having a flight of fancy, or pre-launch jitters. Again, diligence in the Prepare phase (and a good project manager) will help you navigate these conversations.
- **Scope and role creep:** This is anything that puts you on the hook for more work beyond what everyone agreed to at the beginning. You might be able to guess what I'm going to suggest now as a remedy: diligence in the Prepare phase. Fight these battles early on to articulate a clear role and clear assignment. This helps you avoid looking like the defensive jerk who can't be a team player toward the end.

DO THE FINISH WORK

Most of the trades (think: plumbing, carpentry, painting, woodworking) draw a distinction between *rough work* and *finish work*.

Finish work is all the stuff you save until the very end to make sure you won't have to redo it. There's little sense in painting the drywall if you still have to cut a bunch of holes in it to install the electrical.

If you follow the workflow laid out in this book, you will naturally accumulate a list of finish work for your writing. Review your assignment, your draft, and your project notes to compile a fresh checklist of what needs to happen to really be *done*.

Let's look at a few common steps that are best left until the tail end of your writing workflow.

Add links

While you're writing and editing, there are likely links that you want (or *have*) to include in order to make the design function. In earlier phases, you marked those link opportunities, but didn't actually link them, in order to keep your momentum.

But we're not composing anymore, so it's time to find your sources and write those links. First, review your writing for the links you marked, as well as new link opportunities. Some link behavior, like on interface elements such as buttons, has probably been spelled out in the design. For longer informational pieces, like knowledge base articles and blog posts, additional links can increase the usefulness of what you've created.

There's a bit of an art form to linking, especially in longform text. Before social media swallowed the web, there was a very egalitarian spirit of linking any mention of a concept to a good source about that topic. I try to carry that spirit forward in my digital writing, when I can. (Worst case: somebody downstream removes the link.)

Here are some quick guidelines to help you add good links:

- Link complete phrases and ideas. The linked text should make its destination clear (no point in being mysterious).
- Link to the thing the first time it's mentioned in the writing. (It doesn't need to be linked every time.)
- Link to things that support the goals of your design. You don't need to link every noun that your site has a web page for. Consider why readers are looking at that page at all, and what they'll get out of following the link—and whether navigating away to a different page will disrupt a more critical action.
- If the link does anything weird like open a dialog, download a file, reload the page, or open a new window, think very carefully about why that's the case, and include as much context around the link as possible. Your style guide or usability guidelines may have advice on this.

Write and add metadata

As the writer, you're more familiar with the content than anyone else will ever be. This puts you in a good position to decide (or at least recommend) things like appropriate tags and categories, the best place within your site structure to publish the content, and so on. You're also in a good position to write summaries for search engines and social media.

Ideally, you're writing something that's based on a predetermined content type, with all of the metadata required to support that content type already spelled out in advance. In practice, you may find yourself needing to ask questions and poke around inside of systems to determine what metadata is needed.

To oversimplify things, there's going to be two kinds of metadata: public and process. *Public metadata* means stuff that a user or reader might end up seeing, like a page title, search engine summary, author name, or blog category. Public metadata tends to be easier to write at the end of your workflow, since it's based on the final content of whatever you wrote.

Process metadata is stuff that helps your content move through the production workflow, like ID numbers that correspond to a content inventory, or status indicators to track who's reviewed and signed off on the content. You'll need to package all of this stuff up together along with your writing in order to cross that assignment off your to-do list.

Proof it

Proofreading your final drafts is a smart habit to get into, even if what you've written will go through its own dedicated proofing and QA process. Proofing your own writing will help you catch any silly mistakes you'd rather other people not see first, and it helps you learn about your own bad habits and improve upon them.

Make sure the quotation marks are smart, copyright symbols are in place, paragraphs break where you intended, and so on. If you've been working in plain text or otherwise keeping your drafts tidy and clean, you may not have much to clean up. Still, be sure to check for any formatting funkiness and hidden characters that happened while copying and pasting your text into another format.

To guide this process, consider using a personal proofing list: a playbook of sorts for your proofreading process. The list contains words (or parts of words) and phrases that you can search for in your text using the Find feature in your writing environment. It's not a list of dos and don'ts—it's just about seeing your text in a fresh way to make it easier to catch errors.

Some things you might put on your list:

- words you frequently misspell (the misspelled version would go on your list)
- homonyms that trip you up
- typos you can't seem to shake (like "teh")
- marketing and business jargon you want to avoid
- misspellings of product and feature names relevant to your design
- words that represent key topics or pages you want to make sure get linked

- word parts like "ly" and "ing" that can highlight potentially weak writing
- words that are not the preferred synonym for something in your product universe (e.g., if members should "join" instead of "register," you'd put "register" on your list—you can check your controlled vocabulary documentation for things like this.)

You might also include specific steps you want to go through each time before you hand off a draft, such as saving a master copy, alerting someone on your team, or applying formatting that's needed to shepherd it along the project process.

PREPARE FOR THE FUTURE

In addition to the requirements of your assignment and production workflow, there are some personal tasks you'll want to complete to support yourself as a writer and designer. They add some finality to the process, and over time will make it easier for you to get the writing done in the future.

Tidy your desk

Remember how I told you to keep the receipts? Keep that up. Grab a clean copy of that final version and put it in a safe deposit box, so to speak. You want a version that represents every design decision that was made up until the text was out of your hands.

This is to cover your ass, yes, and to save for your portfolio, yes—but it's also because you don't want to have to do anything over again if something gets screwed up when you're no longer minding the store. Projects can stall, stakeholders can leave, designers and developers can screw up. Hopefully you won't ever need your safe deposit copy, but you'll be damn glad to have it if you do.

This is a good habit to get into even if *you* are the next step in the design process. Having a safe copy of the text can help you recover from bad ghost edits—those tiny little changes that you just can't help yourself from making while moving the text from one place to another. Even if it feels minor, you'll want to be able to know what changed from the approved version so you can roll it back if needed.

Keep everything you've written, even if it got thrashed to pieces during editing or review. All that stuff you wrote during this assignment can serve as an input for you on the next assignment. Mindmaps, interview notes, and alternate earlier drafts can all be very valuable.

Write down what you've learned

Writing, like any other thing you might want to get better at, benefits from reflection and review.

So. How did it go?

Whether you use a formal postmortem process with multiple participants, or just a bit of "Remember this next time" journaling on your own, you should reflect on a few key things:

- What changed between articulating and finishing the writing assignment? Why?
- What tools worked well? What tools didn't work well? Why?
- How could you have gotten this work done faster?
- How could you have improved the quality of the writing?
- What do you wish you'd known at the beginning that you know now?
- What is the number one thing you would do differently next time?

There are also a few housekeeping items you'll want to take care of:

- Reflect on the editing phase and update your personal proofing list.

- Send updates and quick notes of thanks to anyone who contributed to the writing, if appropriate (such as SMEs you interviewed and editors you collaborated with).
- Check your various to-do apps and project management tools to make sure everything is checked off.
- Ensure that whoever needed the writing is aware that it's done and ready to roll!

HIT SEND AND BUY YOURSELF A LEGO SET

The absolute last step in all of this—and absolutely do not skip this—is to celebrate. For a big or difficult assignment, I celebrate finishing my work by buying a LEGO set. For smaller assignments, it might be a pint of ice cream. (Note that this is celebration ice cream, distinct from any ice cream consumed while working on the assignment.)

Whether it's ice cream or a LEGO set or going for a run along the river, having a celebration ritual reinforces the idea that you're *done* with the thing and helps move it along out of your brain. Rituals are a way of telling yourself: "The assignment is finished, and I did my best. Good job, me."

Your next writing assignment might be easier, or harder, or bigger, or smaller. I hope you've learned from this experience that you can always get the writing done with a good plan and a bit of perseverance, and by following the four key phases: Prepare, Compose, Edit, and, finally, Finish.

It's a lot to manage, I know. If you find yourself feeling overwhelmed along the way, remember these truths:

1. Writing is part of design. (And being a designer!)
2. Writing is always hard. (I feel your pain.)
3. Workflow gets the writing done. (It ain't magic, just planning.)
4. You can write. (And you did!)

Good job, you!

ACKNOWLEDGMENTS

Writing a book about writing makes one feel especially vulnerable. I couldn't have done it without the skillful guidance, warm encouragement, and A+ edits that Lisa Maria Martin and Katel LeDû provided throughout this process. Thank you Jeffrey Zeldman, Jason Santa Maria, and everyone else at A Book Apart for creating a world where this book can exist alongside so many great titles I rely on in my own work.

I'm honored and grateful to have Dan Brown's name on my cover. He gives generously to the design community in myriad ways and I've grown so much from following his work. I personally recommend reading anything and everything he writes.

To my family, especially Mom, Dad, Aunt Vandie, Uncle George, Jake, and Rob, thank you for your love, and for supporting my early interest in computers and the web, even if you didn't always understand what I was going on about. Thanks Mom and Dad for all the books, all the trips to the library, and for making sure we had a home computer and internet access long before either was common in rural Nebraska.

Many ideas in this book were first developed for a conference talk and workshop. To everyone who shared their time with me in those sessions, asked challenging questions, and provided feedback, thank you.

I'm grateful to everyone who was ever patient with me while I fumbled about trying to figure out my career, especially Fritz Jünker, Amedeo Rossi, Ryan Patrick, Keri Thien, Cat Rocketship, Kathy Landin Hellstern, Neil Roberts, Igor Dobrosavljević, Amanda Morrow, Dan Newman, Agnieszka Skuczynska, and Sara Briddell. I'm still not sure what I want to do when I grow up, but I'm closer thanks to all of you.

To Michael Metts, thank you for your friendship, your encouragement on this project, and for indulging me in various schemes over the years.

Part of everything good I've ever done is for Soro and Gweedo. I miss you both.

Finally, to Kristina Halvorson and my Brain Traffic and Confab family, thank you for making a place for me. I literally and figuratively do not know where I would be without you.

RESOURCES

Sorry, friend, no magic tricks in this section, either. But I *do* have some apps, tools, and further reading that can make the writing work a bit easier (or at least more fun).

Digital writing environments

It's a golden age for writing apps, especially on Mac. Most are relatively inexpensive, especially compared to the big box "productivity suites" of the past. Try out a few to find one that fits your style.

Environments for writing solo

- Drafts (iOS, soon on macOS) is a great place for quickly capturing and manipulating text.
- Ulysses (macOS and iOS) uses a library model (as opposed to files), making it a good place to develop longer writing like blog posts, white papers, and ebooks.
- Byword (macOS and iOS) has a clean and simple plain text writing environment that makes it a nice upgrade from TextEdit.

Environments for writing together

- Google Drive is hard to beat for collaborative writing.
- Dropbox Paper is an alternative to Google.
- Draft is a web-based writing environment focused on version control and collaboration. If I need detailed feedback from one collaborator and don't want to set up a whole new thing, I might drop text into Draft and share it that way.

Reading to improve your writing

Books

- *The Elements of Style* is a surprisingly enjoyable and inspiring read about expressing oneself clearly. It's a classic for a reason.
- *The 10% Solution* is an uncommon little book focused on self-editing your writing. The author brings to bear a perspective on writing for broadcast (e.g., radio commercials) and there are a surprising number of parallels to writing for digital.
- *The Yahoo! Style Guide* has a good chance of outlasting the Yahoo! company. It contains excellent guidance on a number of conventions unique to writing for the web and digital interfaces. When in doubt, I default to the advice in this book.
- *Letting Go of the Words* offers lots of case studies and examples that might inspire your own work writing longform website content.
- *Content Design* would be a great book to pick up right after this one, if you have a lot of content to create. It has simple and clear guidance on how to connect business needs with audience needs in all of your content, and some process tips on approaching text-heavy pages with a design mindset.

Articles

- "The Grammar of Interactivity" introduced me to the "Wilty Wilt test" for evaluating the clarity of interface copy.
- Mary Dash's writing advice on plainlanguage.gov covers a lot of good stuff on active vs. passive voice, modifiers, verb choice, and other writerly matters I didn't get into in this brief text.

Useful utilities

- Pastebot is a clipboard manager that puts multiple levels of copy-and-paste right under your fingers, even allowing you to save frequently used snippets.
- TextExpander is a text replacement app—like autocorrect, except actually useful. Type a few characters and *bloop!* they get automatically expanded into something else. (For instance, `;sig` expands my email signature.) Great for adding consistency to anything you have to type frequently, like URLs, email addresses, and product names.
- Readable.io is an online tool focused on readability tests. You can also run readability tests in Word or in an app like Marked 2. (Remember to use the same readability test in the same app throughout your assignment to ensure accurate results.)
- Terminology is a zippy and well-designed pocket thesaurus/ dictionary. I find this app especially useful when I know what word I want but I can't quite think of it. Great for "namestorming" sessions for products and features, too.

Mindmapping and idea sorting

Mindmapping is a popular app category and there are plenty to choose from. There may be mindmapping functionality built into design software that you already own.

- MindNode (macOS and iOS) is my preferred bare-bones outlining and mindmapping app. I use it on almost every project. I also like to eat peanut butter straight out of the jar. So, you know, it may be best to try out a few and make up your own, uh, mind.
- MindMeister (Web, iOS, Android) is a collaboration-focused mindmapping and diagramming platform.
- OmniGraffle (macOS and iOS) is a simple diagramming tool that can rough out concepts quickly—and make mindmaps in a pinch.
- Trello (Web) is my favorite way to digitally approximate a fresh pack of index cards.

Markdown mastery

Markdown is a popular plain text syntax for writing that's destined for the web—you can quickly mark bulleted lists, headings, and more without having to remove your hands from the keyboard.

- What is Markdown? site by Kirk Strobeck is a good one-stop-shop online guide for understanding Markdown.
- "Markdown: Basics" on Daring Fireball is an introductory guide to the syntax from one of its creators.
- Marked 2 (MacOS) is an incredible Swiss Army knife for web writers. The built-in proofing tools can help highlight weak writing and automate your personal proofing list, and the ability to preview with custom stylesheets makes it easy to "wireframe" pages with just text.
- The Markdown Service Tools by Brett Terpstra are the closest you'll get to a magic trick. Service tools install at the system level, and these in particular allow you to do really handy stuff with text in nearly any application, like automatically cleaning up list formatting, or creating Markdown links from all of your current Safari tabs.

REFERENCES: WRITING FOR DESIGNERS

Shortened URLs are numbered sequentially; the related long URLs are listed below for reference.

Chapter 3

03-01 https://www.plainlanguage.gov/

03-02 http://unsuck-it.com/

Chapter 4

04-01 https://abookapart.com/products/design-is-a-job

Resources

05-01 http://getdrafts.com/

05-02 https://ulysses.app/

05-03 https://bywordapp.com/

05-04 https://drive.google.com/drive/u/0/

05-05 http://paper.dropbox.com/

05-06 https://draftin.com/

05-07 https://www.goodreads.com/book/show/33514.The_Elements_of_Style

05-08 http://www.fairwoodpress.com/catalog/item/7652154/8139852.htm

05-09 https://www.goodreads.com/book/show/6883650-the-yahoo-style-guide

05-10 https://www.goodreads.com/book/show/1135441.Letting_Go_of_the_Words

05-11 https://contentdesign.london/book/

05-12 http://www.uxbooth.com/articles/the-grammar-of-interactivity/

05-13 https://www.plainlanguage.gov/resources/articles/dash-writing-tips/

05-14 https://tapbots.com/pastebot/

05-15 https://textexpander.com/

05-16 https://readable.io/

05-17 https://support.office.com/en-us/article/test-your-document-s-readability-85b4969e-e80a-4777-8dd3-f7fc3c8b3fd2

05-18 https://agiletortoise.com/terminology/

05-19 https://mindnode.com/

05-20 https://www.mindmeister.com/

05-21 https://www.omnigroup.com/omnigraffle

05-22 http://www.trello.com/

05-23 http://kirkstrobeck.github.io/whatismarkdown.com/

05-24 https://daringfireball.net/projects/markdown/basics

05-25 http://marked2app.com/

05-26 http://brettterpstra.com/projects/markdown-service-tools

INDEX: WRITING FOR DESIGNERS

ABOUT THE AUTHOR

Scott Kubie is a designer and digital strategist living in Minneapolis, where he works as lead content strategist at Brain Traffic. His first bit of published writing was a fan letter in the LEGO catalog. Scott can be found online at kubie.co and in person at various grungy rock clubs around the Twin Cities.

Since 2010, Scott has delivered over sixty public talks and workshops on writing, content strategy, and user experience design for audiences of designers, developers, marketers, artists, makers, and more. He loves a good framework and finding ways to make esoteric design topics a bit more practical.

11

A BOOK APART

PRESENTING DESIGN WORK

DONNA SPENCER

FOREWORD BY
DENISE JACOBS

BRIEFS

Publisher: Jeffrey Zeldman
Designer: Jason Santa Maria
Executive director: Katel LeDû
Managing editor: Lisa Maria Marquis
Editors: Sally Kerrigan, Caren Litherland, Danielle Small
Book producer: Ron Bilodeau

ISBN: 978-1-937557-80-5

A Book Apart
New York, New York
http://abookapart.com

TABLE OF CONTENTS: PRESENTING DESIGN WORK

FOREWORD

IF YOU WORK IN the tech industry and have anything to do with design, chances are you've had to present your work to clients or team members at some point. The process can be excruciating: gathering all of the information you think you need to include, practicing (or not) what you plan to say, losing sleep the night before. When presentation day comes, you find yourself in front of a roomful of people—some expectant, some distracted, some disinterested, and some who ask "questions" afterward that invariably seem to derail the conversation.

Presentations have a way of triggering self-doubt. Yes, we want to share our work and help others understand it better, and it's wonderful to have our skills as designers confirmed. But if we feel like our work isn't understood or valued, we can start to wonder whether or not we're cut out for it. If only we were free to do the creative problem-solving we're so good at without having to present it to a tough crowd!

As a professional keynote speaker, author, and former web designer slash front-end developer, I'm intimately familiar with the relationship between creativity, presenting, and self-doubt. And I'm pleased to report that although preparing and giving presentations will probably always seem like a daunting amount of work, Donna Spencer has written a book that will make the process more straightforward and less excruciating.

I first met Donna in 2015 when I keynoted GIANT Conference. She immediately impressed me with her extensive experience, keen smarts, deep knowledge of the UX industry, and fantastic sense of humor. In 2016, I got to know Donna even better when she invited me to keynote UX Australia. It was then that I saw firsthand her deep commitment to strengthening the UX community through creating an event filled with relevant, meaningful content.

This book is a condensed version of much of what I've experienced of Donna as a person—but with a laser-like focus on presenting design work. She has taken her years of experience, love of teaching, and drive to help people work better and has woven them, with great wit and care, into a series of easy-to-follow steps.

There's a common misconception that presenting well stems from natural ability—that polished speakers don't ever doubt themselves or get nervous, and that effective presenters don't need to prepare in advance. Nothing could be further from the truth. Presenting anything well comes from having the right mental approach, knowing the proper steps and structure required to present effectively to an audience, and putting in lots (and lots) of practice.

That's where Donna's book comes in. By pragmatically laying out the steps required to nail any and every design presentation you give, it aims to help you fine-tune your mind-set in a way that will completely transform how you think about and approach presenting design work. This book will benefit not only design professionals who struggle to present their work, but anyone who needs to present creative problem-solving to colleagues and stakeholders.

—Denise Jacobs

INTRODUCTION

EFFECTIVELY PRESENTING WORK IS one of the most important skills a designer can have. It will likely demand almost as much of your time as design itself.

And yet, we aren't usually taught how to do it. It isn't part of most design school curricula (and not all designers went to school anyway). Design books and blogs cover presentation briefly, at best. I, like many others I've talked to, just figured it out as I went along.

Luckily, I'm a natural presenter and storyteller. Standing in front of an audience—small or large—has never been a problem for me. So I didn't really think about how difficult presentations were until I started leading and coaching designers. Only then did I realize that, for most people, presenting work is very stressful and very scary.

I think the stress has two sources. The first comes from the general difficulty of presenting; the second involves a real lack of clarity about *why* we present in the first place.

On the surface, it seems that we present our work to show what we've done—to demonstrate progress, communicate our skills, and present the actual designs. What's less obvious is that presenting isn't actually about presenting. It's more about listening, communicating, and inviting other people into the design process. Showing something off is just a way to win more involvement.

That's why this book focuses on the other people in the room as much as the presenter themselves. While I do, of course, talk about how to present your design work effectively, just as much of the book covers how to get the best out of your audience.

The "design work" I talk about in this book is mostly the sort of work a user will eventually interact with. Think screens, devices, and services. Much of the advice in these pages is relevant to presenting visual branding and research as well, and I've included some suggestions for this in the Resources section.

This little book covers the following:

- The story of a presentation that didn't go well
- Why we present design work
- How to consider the audience and plan to work with them
- How to present the work
- How to prepare, rehearse, and manage the presentation
- How to get great feedback and use it

It's intended as a short, practical book that you can read quickly and use to make immediate improvements to your presentations. If you've felt stressed and frustrated by how your presentations have gone in the past, I hope the advice you find here will help you improve the very next one you give.

1

WHEN PRESENTATIONS GO WRONG

IT'S TUESDAY AFTERNOON: time for the team to present its progress to the client and stakeholders. They've been working on a website for local businesses to promote used and repaired items. Alex, the lead designer, has not been looking forward to this afternoon—it's the third presentation, and she just doesn't seem to be getting through to the clients.

Alex has been worrying about this all day. She finished the slides half an hour ago and got to the meeting room a few minutes early. But now she can't figure out how to show both the slides and the prototype screens; when one is working, the other one won't display properly. Her colleague Josh leans over her shoulder and points to the button that switches it over. Phew! Just in time.

She sees someone she hasn't seen in previous meetings—nicely dressed, with a neat purple blazer—maybe an account manager? She also notices fewer people than last week but can't tell who's missing.

She gets going. "Hi guys—oops, I mean... everyone... thanks for coming. We've done a lot since the last presentation. I'll show you where we got to." She opens up the first screen of the prototype. "Oh, that's not the right screen." Slightly frazzled, she quickly zooms out to find the right one and starts again. Priya, a product manager who has attended all of the meetings so far, begins to feel a little seasick from the rapid on-screen scrolling.

The first version of the homepage features a big search box in the middle, which is what the marketing manager, Grant, advised against in the last meeting; it might be okay for users, but it's not great for the businesses the client is trying to promote. Before Grant can raise his hand to ask about this, though, Alex explains that they've ruled this one out already, and quickly shifts to a second version, with a carousel of product photos. This one, Alex explains, would be great for the businesses, but would not make it easy for users to find what they wanted. Already feeling that the meeting is a waste of time, Grant begins writing notes to prep for his customer calls this afternoon and has mostly tuned out by the time Alex shows the third version, which the team decided was a good mix of the first two.

Alex points out everything visible on the page: the navigation, the dropdown menu at the side of the page, the map that filters location, the carousel of product photos, and the keyword search. Mei, the developer, begins to worry she won't have anything to contribute to this meeting, just like the last one. As Alex changes the screen, Mei seizes the opportunity and interjects, "Carousels don't scale well to mobile—is there a different plan for how mobile displays might work?"

Grant looks up and is struck by the tangerine color used on the page; it reminds him of one of their competitor's apps. "I don't mean to interrupt," he interrupts, "but is this the final color scheme?"

"Hold on, please—I'll take questions at the end." Alex forges ahead. She's lost her train of thought now and stumbles over a few words before remembering what she meant to say. Right, the storefront page. She points out the business logo and business description, and then describes how the products will be displayed on the page. She notices a few people writing notes and shuffling, looking like they're getting ready to talk, so she speeds up to head off any more interruptions.

She quickly moves on to the third screen, which contains details about a product that can be purchased. She points out the large product photo and explains that users will be able to hover over it to get a quick view. She points out the dropdowns to select size and color. She explains that, for users who are logged in, the related products will be personalized based on what they have previously purchased.

Finally, she arrives at the last screen. She got through the presentation! She turns to the group and asks, "What do you think?"

The comments and questions fly back at her:

- "My sister would really love this. How would she add her store to the service?"
- "Are you going to use that font?"
- "Can we make sure people can't narrow down the location too much? We want to make sure as many businesses as possible come up in the results."

- "Are you using AI to improve the recommendations?"
- "Does it work on an iPhone?"
- "Can you make the buttons rounder? They look too square."

Alex scrambles to make some notes. She hadn't anticipated these kinds of questions, most of which don't even seem to be related to what she just showed.

"We've already finished the designs for business sign-up. I showed them during the last meeting." Really, when will Priya let this one go? She's asked some version of this question at every meeting so far. "No, we're not going to use that font. At the moment, we're wireframing the core features; we'll work on the visual approach once the wireframes are signed off." Why are they always asking about the font? It's not important at this point. "We haven't detailed how the location filter will work yet. Yes, the site will work on an iPhone." She ignores the question about AI.

Alex walks out of that presentation feeling frustrated. She's sure the work is good, but the stakeholders didn't react well. Every week, they ask the same questions and give feedback that isn't relevant. She knows she prepared, but she completely forgot to go through the slides she made—it gets so hectic trying to keep ahead of people's questions and comments.

The clients walk out of the presentation feeling frustrated as well. The presentation was too fast for them to understand; it was hard to figure out which screens were the final ones, and they didn't know what they were being asked to look at. They felt like their questions hadn't been answered and still didn't know how to get them answered.

WHEN PRESENTATIONS GO RIGHT

Presentations can be much better than this. Here's what happens in a great presentation:

- The audience understands what's happening and what's expected of them.
- Stakeholders listen, ask smart, relevant questions, and give feedback that's related to their expertise (instead of opinion).
- You feel calm, confident, and in control.
- The entire team walks away able to create a much better product.

But how do we get there? Let's start with understanding why we present our work in the first place.

2

WHY PRESENT DESIGN WORK?

As designers, we present a *lot*. We are constantly showing our work—sometimes to a fellow team member, sometimes to a client. Sometimes it's a casual chat; other times, it's more formal, and the entire success of the project hinges on it.

Why do we do present so much? Why do I suggest it's a core skill for designers?

Ultimately, the reason we share our work is to get broader input. When we get outside our own heads, we stand to learn more about the goals we've set out to achieve. We set ourselves up to make the best possible product or service.

PRESENTING ISN'T ABOUT YOU

Creating a product or service is not a solo undertaking. It belongs to a team—often quite a large one.

- **There is usually someone in a business who owns the overall product.** This person also usually owns the *risk*. They're financially responsible and also responsible for what happens when the product or service goes out into the world. Although designers sometimes think they make the design decisions, ultimately, it's this person who makes final decisions about the design—it's their risk they're managing.
- **There are usually subject-matter experts who know the context in which the product or service will sit.** These people know about legislation and regulations, understand how work actually happens, and grasp the nitty-gritty details of the real world. They will usually have an impressive understanding of unusual situations or requirements. They often know what the edge cases are and what might go wrong.
- **Frontline staff members know about all the situations users find themselves in.** They understand the wide variety of uses a product or service will be put to. They may also be the ones who will ultimately have to deal with any poor design decisions.

- **Developers build digital products.** They have a solid understanding of what is easy to implement and what is hard. Perhaps they have built something similar, so they know what will trip the design up. They appreciate how factors like database efficiency, security, and performance will affect the product. They can offer alternative approaches to achieve the design outcome.

All of these people should play a significant role in the design. They have important and valuable input. They also probably have other jobs, so their only chance to contribute is at presentation time.

Apart from actually creating the design, the main job of a designer is to help other people make good and informed decisions. Designers themselves don't usually get to make final decisions about the product or service—they advise. And they do this via a lot of discussions, a lot of presentations, and a lot of listening.

When I meet designers who express concerns about their presentations, often it's because they feel that presenting is a validation of their value and their skills, which makes it hard not to take criticism very personally.

The best thing I can do for these designers is help remove ego from the equation. Presenting your work is not about getting a pat on the back, validation of your skills, or congratulations for doing well. It's about using the skills and experience of a large, diverse group of people to improve the product or service.

When designers don't think they need to share their work, don't want to ask for feedback, and don't want to make changes as a result of feedback, it shows that there is a problem in the design process. Sometimes designers have a lack of confidence; sometimes, they feel a lot of ownership over the design; sometimes, it's just how they saw designers work in a previous job. Whatever the cause, these designers haven't realized that the whole team owns the design.

TYPES OF PRESENTATIONS

Design presentations are about discussions and decisions. Some presentations lean more toward the discussion end of the spectrum, others more toward the decision end. Each type has a different level of formality and a different kind of feedback process.

Presenting progress

The least formal and most frequent type of presentation is the regular check-in with a project team to discuss progress. If you're working as part of a team on a long-running project, you'll be doing these a lot.

In this kind of presentation, your goal will be to show progress and get ongoing feedback and input from the team. You'll be showing the design itself, asking questions of the team, checking assumptions, and discussing feasibility. You'll definitely be listening more than you'll be presenting.

A regular team should know how the project is tracking and who is responsible for what. You should be able to collect feedback, discuss options, and make decisions on the spot.

Presenting project status

A slightly more formal type of presentation is a regularly scheduled meeting that may be open to a broad group of people, mainly to show the current status of a project. Many Agile teams call this something like *showcase*. If you're working in a consulting capacity (where the project team works together, often offsite), your regular project check-ins will usually be this type.

The goals of this kind of presentation are to show the current state of the design and to collect quality feedback.

Note that I didn't say "show you've made progress" here. In my experience, these sorts of presentations have a revolving group of people who pop in when they can. They don't attend regularly enough to care about progress; they care mostly about the current state of things. Because people attend infrequently, they may want to give feedback on parts of the design that are already resolved, as we saw with Priya's question to Alex about the business sign-up page in the example presentation. (We'll learn more about how to manage infrequent participants in Chapter 3.)

Status presentations focus mainly on the problems the design solves and not so much on the nitty-gritty details of each screen. When thinking about what you're going to present, make sure it clearly demonstrates how it will meet the needs of the business and shows your understanding of the broader goals.

In these presentations, you'll often have limited time, so you'll want to establish a formal feedback mechanism. You might be able to collect and resolve some feedback in the meeting itself, but most will be received and addressed outside the meeting so you can consider it and take action later.

Presenting the final version

When consulting, and sometimes when you're working in-house, there are two contexts in which you'll present a "final" version of a project in a quite formal way: milestones and final presentations.

The goal of these presentations is quite different from those I mentioned above. Here, the goal is to get sign-off. For some milestones, and certainly for a final presentation, the goal is to get paid.

These presentations should be well prepared and well rehearsed.

You should *never* give the first presentation at the same time as you are asking for sign-off. You should also not present anything new at this point. If you present work in progress here, you will be frustrated that you are asked to make changes, and the client will be frustrated that you didn't get it right.

Make it clear upfront that any feedback at this point will inform a follow-up phase of work. Be very clear that you are asking for sign-off (and payment). Don't beat around the bush or avoid the discussion—this is what you are here to do.

Then present a summary of everything you have presented before. Don't add anything new. There should be nothing new to react to and no surprises for the client.

If the client attempts to give feedback, reverse a decision, or ask for additional work (and they will, no matter how well you've presented in the past and how well you've managed feedback), refer back to previous discussions and decisions. Which, of course, you have been documenting and sharing all along.

If something unexpected happens, like a more senior person turning up for the first time and wanting to provide input, reiterate what you have presented in the past, the feedback you've received, and the decisions made as a group. Involve the rest of the group to support these decisions. And during the next round, make sure that senior person is involved throughout.

PRESENT EARLY AND OFTEN

A key thing to remember about presentations is that there should be plenty of them throughout the project.

Some teams make the mistake of having only a few presentations, with the first being after work has been underway for some time. Don't do this—people will feel like they aren't being allowed to contribute, and their feedback can undo a lot of work.

The most common reason for delaying a presentation is the feeling that you don't have enough to show. Typical excuses for few presentations are they take too long and that clients and stakeholders change their minds every time they see new work. If you set up a presentation and feedback process early on and teach the client how to give good feedback, you'll avoid these problems. Your client will get comfortable with you showing them small amounts of work more frequently, the presentations will be fast, and you won't have to manage dramatic changes in direction. The changes that do occur will tend to come earlier and will be easier to handle.

It's also not uncommon for clients to see the first presentation and realize that you are on the wrong track—perhaps because they didn't know what they really needed. You want to catch this as early as you possibly can.

ALEX RETHINKS HER PRESENTATION GOALS

Let's return for a moment to Alex's story from Chapter 1. It sounds like Alex had been presenting often and was interested in asking for feedback. That's a great start!

Her Tuesday meeting was the second type—a fairly formal presentation about current project status that various stakeholders might attend if and when they can. Since Alex hadn't thought about the goal of the presentation, its style, or the precise areas she wanted to cover, it seems like her presentation was very similar to a progress update—a bit too informal for the audience she ended up facing.

Because this was a formal meeting with unexpected participants, Alex should have focused more on the business problems than on individual screens, considered who was there and why, and planned for feedback.

The good news is that Alex's next meeting goes much more smoothly. She thought about the presentation goals, which were to get feedback on the overall approach for the current feature. She shows far fewer screens as a result, and the commentary is much more focused.

Now, let's take a closer look at how to run both the room and the presentation more effectively.

3

THE AUDIENCE

YOU MAY THINK THAT planning your design presentation should be all about figuring out how to show your great design. Yes, that's important—and we'll discuss it more in Chapter 4. But the truly hard part—the part we'd all like to ignore—is planning for the crowd.

Every presentation has an audience, and you have more control over how they react and behave than you think, as long as you're deliberate about it.

PLAN FOR YOUR AUDIENCE

As I mentioned in Chapter 2, different types of meetings have different types of participants. For regular team meetings, you'll usually know everyone and won't be surprised by strangers. For more formal meetings, people you've never met might show up; others might only attend occasionally.

People you already know

When planning your presentation, first think about the people you already know and have had meetings with before. Think about what their role is, what their skills are, and what they are interested in (these things may not be the same). Consider the questions they ask every time and the topics they seem to care most about. For example, Alex should have been able to predict that Mei would ask about performance on mobile and could have explained it before Mei even posed the question.

People you don't know

Because presenting is about listening, you need to know whom you are listening to. If you don't know who is watching your presentation and why, you cannot possibly use their input to achieve the presentation's goals.

Do everything you can ahead of time to find out who will be in the presentation. Find out who has been invited, who has said they can attend, and who has said they can't. Find out what their roles are, how often they'll be involved, and whether they influence or make decisions.

If you're working as a consultant with an external client, don't be afraid to talk to your contact to find out the answers to these questions. It is the professional, organized thing to do.

Sometimes this is difficult, and sometimes people will simply turn up unannounced. That's okay—it doesn't need to fluster you or mess up your presentation. Always leave time at the beginning of the presentation or meeting to see who is in the room and figure out why they are there. If you find yourself in a room with people you don't know, ask for introductions. Yes, they might already know one another, but you can't present effectively if *you* don't know who is there and what matters to them.

People new to the project

If you know someone new to the project will be attending a presentation, arrange to meet with them beforehand, and show them everything you've covered in previous presentations. That way, they won't disrupt the presentation by asking questions or giving feedback on features that have been finalized.

People who aren't in attendance

There are a number of reasons why people can't attend a presentation. If you know someone can't make it (and they are a key subject-matter expert or decision-maker), arrange to catch up with them outside the presentation. Give them the opportunity to hear the same presentation as everyone else and to deliver feedback in the same way.

Often, someone will attend your presentation, go back to their team to share what they learned, and collect feedback from their group. This can make feedback more difficult. They will never be able to present like you can—they won't understand the details to the same extent, and they don't know where to focus. They probably won't be able to answer questions from their team. Usually, the feedback that trickles back in this manner is neither useful nor usable.

Consider whether you can present to these people directly. That might mean you need to present more often to smaller groups, but it will also mean you get much better feedback and input. If I simply cannot present to people (which I find often happens in healthcare and customer support), I record a short video or give them a set of scenarios and a clickable prototype. It's not the same as talking directly, but it's better than second-hand feedback.

People who are disruptive

Admittedly, it's not easy to plan for disruptive participants. The two types I see most often are people who have a position to push and people who want to revisit decisions that have already been finalized.

If you know who will be there and understand what matters to them, you're already somewhat prepared. If you've arranged to talk to new people or people who missed a presentation, that goes a long way as well. Giving everyone a clear role in the presentation (which I'll discuss in the next section) will also help a lot.

People tend to revisit decisions either when they are made too quickly, without enough reflection and discussion, or when they feel like they haven't been heard. They will derail your presentations until their feedback is considered. If this happens to you a lot, look at how you are collecting feedback, and ask yourself whether you are giving people enough time to reflect and contribute. (We'll cover feedback in more detail in chapter 6.)

PREPARE THE AUDIENCE

Once you have a sense of who will be in the presentation and why, you can be very deliberate about how you involve them in the presentation.

Give people a job

One of the biggest mistakes designers make when they present is giving participants free rein to offer feedback and ask questions about whatever they like—regardless of whether or not they know anything about the topic.

When you show a design and ask for feedback, people will give feedback. Their feedback may or may not be related to any expertise they have—could be an opinion, or could be a random thought. Very few people have the confidence to say, "I don't think I can offer anything here" or "Looks good to me." Almost everyone will feel they need to contribute. And the more senior they are, the more they will feel this pressure.

This is why a lot of feedback is not useful or usable. It's why people will comment on the color or the font or suggest that the corners on the button should be rounder. They just feel the need to say *something*.

Prepare for this by giving people clear instructions on what their role in the presentation is and what you do and don't want to know about. When you give people a job to do, they'll focus on that.

If your audience is made up of representatives from different roles (e.g., project sponsors, managers, developers, other designers), you might be able to give them jobs that relate to their specific role and expertise. Try to avoid stereotyping and pigeonholing them, though—think about what their skills and interests are as well, since most people have expertise outside of their role description.

If your audience is made up of a particular kind of role (e.g., all front-line staff), give them all the same jobs to do, but still be specific about what they should focus on. And of course, if you have a mix, adapt the approach to your actual audience.

The key thing is to give everyone something specific to think about and to emphasize that you want their expertise.

Examples of what you might ask people to focus on include questions like these:

- Will this design work for the core user group and core tasks?
- Will the design work for the content?

- Is there terminology that users won't understand?
- Are there user tasks / edge cases the design won't work for?
- Is there anything technically difficult we haven't considered?
- Is there overlap with work being done by another team?
- Does the design adhere to brand guidelines or the style guide?

This doesn't need to take long. You can do it verbally or make it a slide in a presentation. Decide how formal you want to be based on how long you've worked with a given group.

The most important time to get this right is during your first presentation to a group or the first time a new stakeholder is involved. This is the crucial moment to teach people that they have a specific role and that you want them to contribute their expertise, not their opinions.

Explain the feedback process

Before you start on the presentation itself, take a moment to explain how the feedback process will work. This helps people understand how to participate in the presentation and what they should do. It also lets them know that you are listening and that you value their contribution.

If this presentation is the first in a project or the first for a group, or if you are introducing a new feedback process, take extra time with this. Most people haven't been involved in such a deliberate, structured feedback process before, and it's such an important part of the presentation experience as a whole that it's worth emphasizing.

Explain the presentation process

Let people know how the presentation will be structured—ideally, that you'll run through the whole thing and then discuss it at the end.

People usually only interrupt because they're worried they won't get an opportunity to contribute. I've noticed that if they know there's time for questions at the end, they pay more attention to the presentation, since they aren't wasting mental energy trying to figure out how to insert themselves.

Set the context

Let people know what is in and out of scope—what you'll be discussing, what you won't be discussing, and why you will or won't be discussing those things. When context and scope aren't clear, people don't know where they are meant to focus. They go back over things that have already been discussed or jump ahead to things that aren't yet relevant.

First, explain where you are in the project timeline—what has happened before and what will happen later. Are you 30 percent done or 90 percent done? Next, let them know what you will cover in this presentation—the features, screens, or user tasks. Then tell them what you will not cover.

If it is relevant, remind the group of what you've collectively decided before. Be very clear about this so they know not to go there again.

Then, reiterate what the scope of the presentation is and what you'll be covering. Yes, I deliberately said that twice.

ALEX INTRODUCES HERSELF AT LAST

We didn't see the steps Alex followed to prepare for the Tuesday meeting, but it sounds like she didn't think at all about who would be there. She spotted someone she'd never seen before, as well as another person whose role wasn't clear to her.

For this week's meeting, Alex checks the invite to see who is likely to attend. She notices that Grant has said no, and makes a mental note to reach out to him after the meeting. She sees that someone called Grace is planning to come, and wonders if that was the person in the purple blazer.

As it happens, the mysterious woman is in the meeting again (this time in a green blazer). Alex goes up to her with her hand outstretched for a handshake and says, "Thanks for coming! I'm not sure we've met. I'm Alex, the designer on the team." The woman smiles immediately. "Hi! I'm Grace. I'm from legal."

Alex starts the meeting by greeting everyone and thanking them for attending. "We're going to do something a bit different this week," she says. "Instead of general feedback, I'd like for you to keep an eye on specific things in the design." Because she hasn't yet learned about people's particular concerns, she decides to ask everyone to focus on the same questions, except for one technical question for Mei. She shows a slide containing the following questions:

- Will local shoppers understand, at a glance, what the service is offering?
- Will local shoppers find the homepage interesting enough to click through to explore a product?
- Will the service give local businesses enough exposure that they will be likely to sign up?
- Is there anything that seems technically difficult? (Mei)

Alex explains that she'll run through the designs quickly and will take questions at the end. She adds that they're just going to be focusing on how people can get to the product pages today and that they'll look at that page in more detail next week.

And now that she has prepared for her audience, she can proceed to the heart of the matter: the presentation.

4

THE PRESENTATION

YOU'VE PREPARED FOR YOUR audience; now you're ready to present your work. This will usually make up the bulk of the presentation, and it's your chance to make the design come to life.

EXPLAIN THE PROBLEM YOU ARE SOLVING

Before you dive into the design, describe the problem you are trying to solve. This does two things: it reinforces the scope and context for the design work and helps the audience focus on what the problem is.

Describe both sides of the problem: the business and user problem, using the same sequence your client uses. If they usually talk about the user problem they are trying to solve, start with that. If they typically talk about the business problem they are trying to solve, start with that. But make sure you cover both sides of the problem. In Alex's example, the people in the meeting always talk about how to promote local businesses that sell secondhand products, so she knows that she should first reinforce that she understands what they are trying to do.

This doesn't need to take very long, but it is important to show that you do understand the problem you're solving and that you have been designing for it.

If you're not clear what business and user problems you are trying to solve, do get clarification before you present. Ideally, you'll have this sorted out before you start designing, but we've all worked on projects that seemed unclear or where the business and user problems didn't align. If you really can't get clarification, explain the problems as best you can—your presentation might trigger the discussion that needs to happen to make things clearer. If you're worried that you won't be able to explain the issues well and it will reflect badly on you, see if you can get someone more senior to do the explaining—after all, someone must have had at least an idea of what the project was set up to do.

START WITH THE END RESULT

When you present your design, the most important thing to show is the result you came up with.

"Of course," you say. "That's obvious."

Unfortunately, it isn't obvious. The single biggest mistake I see designers make—just like Alex did—is that they explain their process, show each version of the design they attempted, and discuss every thought, tangent, and rabbit hole they've explored since the last catch-up.

The single biggest improvement is to flip that around and just show the final result.

I understand why designers present their process. They've done a lot of hard work, solved difficult design issues, tried out different approaches, failed, and thrown away ideas. It has been hard—it took *ages* to come up with something that they now know is good and simple and elegant. All of that is top of mind.

But the people hearing the presentation don't care. All they are hearing is: "I thought this thing, then I changed my mind, and this was hard." Like Mei, who felt impatient during Alex's first presentation, they just want you to get to the point.

If stakeholders have questions about alternate approaches or why you didn't do something in a particular way, they'll ask you. In fact, the explanation will make more sense to them when it's given as an answer to a specific question.

"But I need to show my value," designers often tell me, "and talking through my process and what I explored is how I do that." To that I say: The end result *is* your value. It really shouldn't matter whether the design you have created took a day or two weeks—if the solution is good, you are providing value. If you can explain why it's good in the context of the problem it is solving, you are providing value. (Yes, I know a lot of us work in environments where we count hours, not value, but that still doesn't mean you should explain every thought you've had).

So back to the obvious statement. The first thing you should show in your presentation is the result you came up with.

SHOW A PERSON DOING A THING

But how do you show this brilliant result? You demonstrate it as *a person doing a thing*. From the user's point of view.

Start with the most common user scenario for the design. Work through an end-to-end story, starting with the user's goal and ending with them completing the task (or getting as far as they can with what you've designed). Describe it from the perspective of an actual person. Give them a name and a back story; don't just talk about "the user." For example, Alex could bring her presentation to life by introducing Norton, the father of a three-year-old, who needs to buy new clothes for his child. Because kids grow out of their clothes so fast, Norton likes buying (and potentially selling) items secondhand. Alex can show how Norton goes to the homepage, finds stores in his local area with children's clothes, and checks out a few to see what their range looks like.

Present the scenario in one go without interruption. If you stop and point things out along the way, people will start to focus on specific features instead of the overall story.

Next, present a similar task, again from the user's perspective. Start with their goal, demonstrate the workflow, and finish with them completing the task. This time around, Alex could show Norton looking for secondhand vinyl records for himself.

I suggest starting with two core tasks that are quite similar. If some steps are repeated in both scenarios, just repeat them. Show the whole experience both times. This might feel repetitive to you, but it won't feel that way to the audience. The first time will be too quick to take it in. The second time, they can look for the things they are wondering about.

When you've covered the core user tasks, show how the experience might be similar or different for people with different needs or skills. This is a great opportunity to remind people that users are not one-size-fits-all, but have different skills and use different technologies. Demonstrate how the experience sounds to a screen reader. Show what it looks like for someone with their screen zoomed all the way in. Show what it looks like in high-contrast mode. Show how it changes when people use it on different devices or screen sizes. For example, Alex could show how the service works on mobile while Norton is out and about or for someone with limited vision using a screen reader.

Only once you've been through the flow a few times, go back to the start and explain anything you need to cover in more depth. This is the time to point out features you didn't explain when you went through the user flow, explain how those features address business goals, and discuss concerns from particular stakeholders before they ask about them. This is also a good time to explain how user research or testing contributed to the design.

Why focusing on the user works

One reason demonstrating from a user's perspective works well is that it forms a narrative. People love listening to stories, and stories stick in their memory.

Another bonus is that it puts the user at the center of the story and focuses on them. It gives you the opportunity to communicate what matters to users with a clear and engaging story. A user-focused story doesn't talk about features or screen elements, and discourages the audience from focusing on those, too.

Once your audience realizes you are going to present in this narrative form, they'll interrupt less and listen to the story more. Over time, they'll also ask much better questions and will start to ask questions from a user's perspective.

The thing you absolutely, positively must not do is a *real-estate tour*—that is, a screen-by-screen walk-through of a page while pointing out its features. Alex did this during her first presentation. A walk-through doesn't put the screens in the context of a person doing a thing. It draws attention to the features instead of the tasks or benefits and will earn you detailed questions and feedback about the elements on the screen instead of the overall task.

What if my work isn't screens or a user flow?

Occasionally your design work will consist of something more abstract (like a sitemap) or more detailed (like copy). These two examples don't really fit the "person doing a thing" idea. So how do you present them?

This is where you really need to have a clear idea of what your goals are and whether a presentation is the right way to achieve them. Why would you present a sitemap without any user task to support it? Same with copy—why would you present that without a user task? What are you trying to achieve by showing these off?

In my experience, these two types of design work are the most difficult to get feedback and agreement on, simply because audiences have a hard time imagining how such work will eventually be represented, and how users will interact with it. When I've seen designers ask for sign-off for this type of work without something visual to support it, they always end up frustrated when the client changes their mind after seeing the ideas represented in a more tangible form.

I suggest you never present things like this as standalone design work—only present how they affect a person doing a thing. Only then will you be able to have a productive conversation about them.

DON'T USE JARGON

Another advantage of demonstrating a person doing a thing is that when you focus on the user task, you will naturally be less likely to talk about the design-geek elements on the screen. Jargon is such a habitual part of human communication that it's worth attempting to avoid it when talking with people outside your discipline. Did you even notice that Alex used jargon like *dropdown*, *filter*, *carousel*, *hover*, and *personalization*? If you didn't, that's probably because you use these terms without thinking.

Think about what your audience know and understand. If you use terms they don't understand or find relevant, they'll switch off, feel stupid, or contribute their uninformed opinion—none of which will give you the feedback you need.

Just use plain, simple language. Explain clearly. Help your audience understand what they don't know.

A COMPELLING STORY PUTS THE DESIGN IN PERSPECTIVE

For this week's presentation, Alex first describes the business problem the team has been solving (promoting local businesses that sell secondhand products) to show that the team understands both the business and user needs.

Then, instead of showing three different versions of the design and explaining that only the last one was what they decided on, she shows only the final one. This gets the presentation off to a much stronger start by connecting the design to the problem immediately, without irrelevant screens in between.

Instead of pointing out the features on each page, Alex talks about Norton, the father we met earlier. She first shows Norton looking for clothes for his three-year-old child; then looking for vinyl for himself. Next, she demonstrates what the experience would sound like if it were read out by a screen reader, reminding the audience that not everyone uses the service the same way.

With these stories, the audience gets a good, intuitive understanding of the service, and—unlike an overly detailed, blow-by-blow tour—it only takes a few minutes.

Alex then returns to the first page and talks about the various kinds of products available, and shows different ways for people to select the location. She also shares how users have reacted to the designs.

When she opens up for feedback and discussion, the audience members are in the mindset of the user and have been paying attention to what they were asked. Their questions and feedback are a lot more focused and relevant.

The presentation is what the audience sees. What they don't see is all of the work behind the scenes that makes the presentation run smoothly. A little planning goes a long way. We'll take a look at that next.

5

PRESENTATION LOGISTICS

GOOD PLANNING WILL HELP your presentations run smoothly and make them feel much more comfortable—not just for you but for everyone attending. Give yourself enough time for this step, particularly for assembling the presentation and rehearsing it.

PLANNING WHAT TO PRESENT

When thinking about what you'll present, consider the goals of the presentation and what feedback you need.

If you're presenting progress to your team, you might want to present with your working designs, so the team can see and respond to the changes you've made since the last check-in. If you are presenting status in a more formal setting, you'll probably have to make something specifically for that audience, so you don't accidentally show messy work in progress.

Present in the lowest fidelity that will achieve the presentation's goals. People will give feedback on what they see (even when you prepare well by giving people jobs and describing scope). If people see a beautiful, full-color, high-fidelity design with great images, that's what they'll give feedback on, and you'll lose valuable time talking about visuals when you really wanted to talk about the user flow.

If you want feedback on flow and content, show the design without imagery and color. This is a perfect time to show a rough sketch or a black-and-white wireframe. People who have never seen a wireframe before might wonder what they are looking at. You can reassure them that they aren't looking at a terrible final design by showing before-and-after images from a different project that also had a wireframing phase; people usually only need a small example to understand what wireframing is.

If you want feedback on layout, use some version of fake content, so people don't get caught up in the details of what the in-progress copy says. For years I've been using text from classic fiction (like *Alice in Wonderland*)—it's less confusing than lorem ipsum, and people usually smile at it and understand it.

Of course, if you want feedback on the imagery, color, transitions, and interactions, show them!

What you definitely shouldn't present is an already-built design. Not only is it harder to make changes to something that has been built, but it also communicates to your audience that you are not listening to feedback.

PLANNING THE PRESENTATION FORMAT

Consider what technology will best achieve your presentation goals. You might walk through your designs in the original software you used to build them, or you might assemble a more polished slideshow presentation using a tool like PowerPoint or Keynote.

Think about whether you want control or flexibility, how you will ask people to provide feedback (which we discuss in the next chapter), and what you might need to send to people afterward.

A presentation in your favorite presentation tool:

- is good if you like to be organized and plan ahead;
- helps you stick to the flow of your planned presentation;
- is easier to rehearse;
- takes time to prepare;
- isn't as flexible: you can't show something else if someone asks a question;
- can include additional supporting materials such as research results and project progress; and
- is a good record of what was presented and easier to share with people for later review.

A wireframe or prototype demonstration:

- is good if you prefer to be flexible;

- must be set up with care and attention to detail, so you can smoothly navigate through it—if you provide the audience with a prototype link, all screens must be linked together, so people will be able to click through them easily;
- takes time to prepare—you'll want to create a version separate from your working file;
- requires rehearsal, so you know the scenarios work well; and
- may need an additional deck or document to support it with research results or project information.

Planning the next presentation

Start preparing the next presentation as soon as you finish this one. Consider what you want to get out of the next presentation, then arrange the design work in between to meet those goals. This ensures you are focused on getting involvement and feedback, and your design work is directed towards that.

Also, think about the timing and feedback cycle—if it's going to take time to collect and decide on feedback, but you have another presentation due soon, you might need to work on completely different features, so you have time to address previous feedback.

GETTING SUPPORT: DELEGATION AND NOTE-TAKING

Presenting can be a busy and intense experience. You're trying to manage equipment, tell your story, click through screens, observe the audience, and manage questions. It can be very helpful to have a second person to help out with a couple of those tasks, so you aren't juggling them all on your own.

The first job you might consider delegating is to have someone else manage the technology—not just setting it up, but also clicking through the presentation or navigating screens in the prototype as you take on the role of narrator. It's easier to tell a convincing, clear story if you can focus on the people you're talking to.

Note-taking is another area where a helper can be valuable since the process is likely to otherwise interrupt the flow of your presentation and your question-and-answer session. Notes are crucial for remembering what happened in the presentation and ensure you don't later forget to address issues that came up.

You may have a colleague who can support you here (and you can return the favor during their presentations). If not, you may be able to ask someone in the audience to make notes for you. Arrange this ahead of time, so you can let them know how much detail you need and what format the notes will be in. And please, don't default to asking the most junior woman in the room!

If you can't arrange for any note-taking support, consider recording the meeting. I've found that people usually don't mind as long as I tell them ahead of time and explain that I'm recording, so I don't miss anything important. This may even be your default for remote presentations, where you may not need someone to take notes at all. Instead, you can record the presentation and watch it later to make note of the questions people asked.

If you do record the presentation, you can also use that to improve your presentation skills. Go through the recording later, note what went well and what you'd like to improve, and build those learnings into your next presentation. Many people hate hearing or watching themselves, but it is an excellent learning tool.

REHEARSING

Practice your presentation all the way through at least once. This will help you smooth out any uneven sections that might otherwise throw you off course or fluster you when you present for real. Make sure you have your user scenarios straight, and that the presentation, wireframes, or prototype work smoothly for all of your scenarios. Think of questions that people are most likely to ask and make sure you can easily provide answers to them.

Rehearse out loud, even if it feels ridiculous. It's an important presenting trick for your brain: when you've already heard yourself say something, it's easier to do it again later on and sound more confident.

If you'll have someone helping you with the presentation, rehearse with them. This is essential if you'll be asking them to manage the technology, since it takes a couple of run-throughs to get a sense of timing and smooth out any transitions.

If you'll be in an unfamiliar room, check it out ahead of time and find out how everything works. Where are the electrical outlets? How do the light switches work? How long does it take for the projector to warm up? And always carry your own set of adapters—the room will never have the right one at the right time.

Remote presentations have an additional rehearsal overhead; you may need to practice screen-sharing or switching from video to a presentation. Make sure you know how to read and answer written comments. Some screen-sharing applications allow participants to "raise their hand" to ask a question; make sure you know how this works and how to manage it. You don't want to be learning the tool and presenting with it at the same time.

MANAGING THE ROOM

It used to be the norm to present face to face. After all, being in a room with people allows you to connect with the audience and is great when the group has to work together to make decisions.

However, it's becoming easier and more common to present remotely. Remote presentations can be challenging because they make it harder to interact with the group. Also, many people struggle to ask questions or offer feedback during a remote presentation, so anticipate less feedback and discussion during the presentation and perhaps more afterward.

For any kind of presentation, success largely depends on how well you manage the room—physical or virtual.

Owning the room

People find it hard to ignore someone moving around at the front of a room. Our peripheral vision is wired to look up when we see movement, and our social norms have conditioned us to pay attention to the person at the front. If you stand up at the front, move, and gesture, people will look at you.

When you can, present on your feet. Own the room and take up space. Move your arms and gesture. Don't huddle behind the computer—without your physical presence, it's easy for people to get distracted.

Remotely, it may be harder to stand up since you need to remain in view of the camera (though if you can swing it, standing will improve your presence). Make a conscious effort to sit up tall, with good posture—you'll get almost the same benefits as if you were standing up and presenting in person. Sitting up tall makes it easier to get into a pose that makes you feel confident. Breathing is easier if you have your chest open. You can gesture more easily.

Use your voice

Using your body is one way to own a room. Using your voice is another. Use intonation, volume, and expressiveness to tell your stories and emphasize your points.

If this isn't your natural presentation style, rehearse. You'll feel a bit silly doing it, but projecting your voice will really help you keep the audience's attention.

ALEX ASKS FOR HELP

After venting about the last presentation to her colleague Josh, he offers to help Alex so she can focus more on presenting smoothly. By rehearsing together and looking over the prototype, they catch a couple of mistakes that might have thrown her off before. As a result, she goes into the next presentation much calmer—which comes across to the audience too.

Josh also volunteers to take notes during the meeting, which takes a lot of pressure off Alex since she can now fully focus on questions that come up without having to scramble. With both hands free, Alex is able to use her whole body to bring Norton's story to life by acting it out a bit. This also makes for an engaging and memorable presentation, and the audience respects her time much more as a result. They don't interrupt to ask irrelevant questions, because they're more interested to hear what she has to say next.

Alex has come a long way in improving and refining her presentations. But no presentation is complete without feedback; in fact, that's arguably the most important part. There's an art to giving it and getting it. Let's take a closer look.

6

FEEDBACK

THIS IS THE MOST IMPORTANT chapter of the book! After all, the primary reason for presenting design work is not to show off how amazing you are, but to get input from other people, so you can make the product or service even better.

I'm sure you've been in situations like the one Alex found herself in at the beginning of the book—you've asked for feedback and received a bunch of seemingly random, conflicting comments and opinions that were difficult to address and didn't move the product forward. Or perhaps you just felt that you weren't being heard or were being attacked.

Rethinking how you set up the presentation (covered in Chapters 3 and 4) will put you on the right track. Giving people something specific to address keeps them focused on their expertise, explaining the scope clearly focuses them on what you want feedback on, and showing a person doing a thing focuses on the user, not on the features or screen elements.

The other important aspect, which we'll get into now, is *teaching* people how to give good feedback.

Good feedback isn't the same thing as praise. Good feedback is feedback you can use to move the product or service forward. It is:

- concrete,
- actionable,
- specific (with examples),
- detailed and clear, and
- based on the person's expertise.

The best way to get this kind of feedback is to teach your stakeholders how to give it. And the best way to do that is with a consistent structure and examples.

A SIMPLE FEEDBACK STRUCTURE

Once you've presented the design, you'll transition to the "time for questions" that you likely already promised would come at the end. Now that we're here, don't forget that you're still in charge of the presentation. Guide the feedback portion with a few key steps:

1. **Remind your audience what the scope is (and isn't).** "Remember, today we're focusing on how people will get to the product page. We'll go through the product page itself in detail next time."
2. **Remind them of the jobs you gave them and what they should focus on.** "Priya and Grant, do you think this will give local businesses enough exposure that they will be likely to sign up?"
3. **Add some general questions, like these:**
    - "What are you most looking forward to?" This prompts specifically for positive feedback, which you may not get unless you ask for it.
    - "Is there anything that could become a problem?"
    - "Was there anything that you expected to see today that I didn't cover?"
4. **Ask people to provide examples to support their comments.** "I'm glad to hear you find this more straightforward! Which elements, in particular, do you think are making this a better experience for businesses?"

Note that none of the questions above use the word "like." Never, ever ask ,"What do you think?" or "Do you like it?" You will not get concrete, useful feedback with these questions.

COLLECTING FEEDBACK

You have two options for when to collect feedback—you can either take it at the time of the presentation or get people to give it to you later. There are significant pros and cons to both approaches, so consider how each option might affect the kind of feedback you will get.

Feedback during the presentation

It's great to be able to give a presentation, get feedback while everyone is still present, and collectively discuss and resolve what to do about it. It's collaborative and fast, allowing you to keep the project moving at a good pace. Stakeholders can work together to discuss and make decisions, and have conversations they otherwise wouldn't have. You can literally walk out and start using that feedback in your next phase of work, with clear, agreed-upon direction.

But when I say you will be collecting feedback during the presentation, I mean *at the end of* your part of the presentation. I strongly suggest you don't take feedback while you're presenting. It breaks the flow of your narrative, and you lose some control of the story. Let people know that you'll take feedback at the end, and they'll usually hold off asking questions while you're presenting. If they do ask a question, let them know that you'll come back to it, and continue the presentation. Do make sure you come back to them, though, or they won't trust that they'll be heard.

You will need to plan a note-taking method and explain to people what they should do before you present your work. An easy method is to ask people to use sticky notes to record their comments. Then at the end, the group puts the sticky notes on a wall, groups them thematically, and discusses them. This is often called *affinity diagramming*.

Another approach is to have a discussion after the presentation and record the discussion on a whiteboard while you talk about it. This helps people understand that you are listening, that their ideas have been noted, and they can see what decisions the group makes.

Don't ever just have a chat with no visibility about decisions. This makes people feel like you are not listening to them, and they'll be reluctant to contribute later.

Feedback after the presentation

Often there is just not enough time to get feedback on issues in any depth during the presentation. You've shown something to people, asked them to think of issues on the spot, and resolved them quickly. When I've been a stakeholder in this type of situation, I later think about all of the other things that are going to matter and that we didn't get to discuss.

This can be why people often want to discuss things you think you've resolved: You haven't given them the opportunity to reflect properly on what they saw so that they can contribute well. If you don't give people enough time to contribute, they will derail your presentations until their feedback is addressed.

My preference for anything of reasonable complexity is to allow people time to think and provide good feedback. It's slower, but the feedback is infinitely better, more useful, and will lead to a much better product or service.

After the presentation, always send people a message with clear instructions around what you want them to do and how they should do it. Don't rely on people to remember what they've agreed to. Give them a deadline and follow up a few days before the deadline.

Let people give you feedback in a way that is easiest for them, not easiest for you. If you put the burden on them, they either won't do it or will do it poorly. You can offer:

- email,
- a questionnaire,
- a phone call or chat, or
- leaving comments electronically on the prototype.

Then, use whatever organizational system works well for you to track responses. A spreadsheet, document, or database might be all you need. Or you can use bug-tracking or project-tracking software. Just don't lose any feedback.

A potential issue with giving people time to answer is that they will go back to their teams and get feedback from a broader group. This should be a good thing—broader feedback is better for making sure you've uncovered and addressed issues. Do what you can to reach these folks effectively, as covered in Chapter 3, so that their feedback is useful.

Feedback without a presentation

A common approach to showing design work is to send your designs to the client and have them write back to you with questions and feedback. Technology makes this easy; many design tools give you the ability to easily add comments and reply to them within the tool.

This will never be as good as presenting in person (or presenting remotely in person), but it works reasonably well when:

- the design is simple enough that it can be interpreted without a lot of explanation,
- you already have a strong relationship with the client,
- you have taught them how to give good feedback,
- you have taught them how to interpret the designs, and
- you have taught them how to use the software—both for clicking through for a scenario and for leaving comments.

In this case, you'll want to make sure that along with the design files, you send a well-written description covering everything I've suggested you do in person:

- Clarify people's roles and give them particular things to focus on.
- Tell them which parts of the design to focus on and which are out of scope.
- Write out a set of user scenarios that they can follow through themselves.
- Remind them to look at the design at different screen sizes if that's relevant.

Be sure to give them a clear description of when and how to get feedback back to you, too.

Always ask for feedback

Should you ever show a design and not ask for feedback? For example, just to show that you have made progress?

I'd suggest not doing that. It's unsatisfying for stakeholders to see work in progress without being able to react to it. It makes them feel like you aren't listening and that they can't contribute. Either make sure you have something to get feedback on or wait until you do.

If you feel like you need to show progress to prove that you are working, consider how you structure your work—why is there nothing you can get feedback on?

MAKING DECISIONS

Whether you collect feedback during the presentation or later, you need to decide what to do with all of it.

I find that feedback falls into five categories:

Agree and now

Much of the feedback will be simple changes that the team understands, agrees with, and can be done relatively soon. They go into your to-do list to implement quickly.

Agree and later

Some of the feedback will relate to issues that the team does need to incorporate, but they can't be acted on immediately. These will go into a backlog or added as a feature for later. This category tells people that you are listening and acknowledging that you are going to do something about their requests.

Needs research

Some feedback will be for issues where you don't have enough information to make a decision. They may need some other kind of input, such as:

- additional research with users,
- additional discussion with stakeholders or subject matter experts (beyond clarifications),
- content analysis, or
- analysis of analytics.

Add the research aspect of these into your backlog, and again, let people know that you have listened and will be acting on their feedback.

Clarify

People will often give you feedback that you just don't understand, especially when you take feedback after the presentation. Clarify such feedback quickly and add the clarification into one of the other categories.

No

This is the hardest and most important category.

I think most designers (and product teams) do this particularly poorly, and it can be the main reason stakeholders stop engaging or give the same feedback endlessly.

You must be able to explain why you have decided not to do something about feedback people have given you.

It's relatively easy when they have given you poor-quality feedback: there are usually good reasons why you won't change the color palette or the roundness of the corners on a button.

It's much harder when people have given you high-quality feedback. You have to listen, understand, reflect, and have clear reasons why you aren't going to do something about it. It adds another level of rigor to your decision-making. This is a good thing, but it takes experience and confidence to be able to do it. And it's even harder when you're face-to-face with someone (another advantage of collecting feedback and dealing with it later).

COMMUNICATE IT BACK

After all this good work deciding what feedback you'll act on and what you won't (and why), make sure you communicate this back to stakeholders.

This is the very best way to build up long-term trust. Your audience will know that you've listened to them. They'll learn about what's easy, what's hard, and why. You'll learn more about their actual concerns and constraints.

How you'll do this depends on how your team is set up. You can arrange a meeting to discuss the feedback and issues (particularly around the "no" questions) and collectively make decisions. Once the team is working well together and trusts that you are listening, you can simply email a summary of feedback and decisions. If you store feedback and decisions in a tracking system, you may be able to give everyone access to it.

I suggest you don't address feedback and present new information in the same meeting. Discussing feedback can be difficult. Keep feedback and new work separate. It will also feel like you haven't listened if you are presenting something new before addressing previous issues.

ALEX USES A STRUCTURED FEEDBACK PROCESS

In her last presentation, Alex tried to make some notes and answer questions on the spot.

This time, she plans the feedback process in advance. She takes a few questions in the meeting, answering the simple ones. Josh makes a note of those that need to be followed up on. She lets everyone know she'll send them the slides, so they can go through them in more detail. Then, she asks them to get feedback to her by Friday. Later that day, she emails everyone a follow-up as promised.

When the feedback comes in, she arranges a meeting with the team to go through it and decide what to do about it. They make decisions about changes that are straightforward, and they add some jobs to the backlog for other tasks. One item is out of scope for the project, so they agree not to act on it. Alex prepares a summary of their decisions and sends it to the client, showing them that everything has been considered and letting them know when they can expect to see it incorporated into the designs.

The clients are much happier overall. They know that they contributed and that their contributions were considered, and they're able to understand the reasons behind the project team's decisions, which gives them confidence in the team.

After a few rounds of this presentation and feedback process, the whole team (including the client and stakeholders) are now working very effectively. They are listening to each other and reaching out more to discuss aspects of the design. Questions and comments are very focused, and no one ever asks about a font or the shape of a button. The whole team talks in terms of a person doing a thing.

This is achievable for your projects as well. It may not happen immediately, as you, your team, and your clients may all have to learn a new way of working together. But it will happen faster than you imagined.

CONCLUSION

IF I HAD TO SUMMARIZE my key points in a single presentation slide—well, I wouldn't. I'd make five slides, each containing one strong point:

1. If you plan for your audience and give everyone a job, they'll contribute their expertise, not their opinion.
2. If you show the end result, not your progress or process, your audience will understand what you are showing them and won't get distracted by process details.
3. If you present a person doing a thing and tell a compelling story, your audience will give feedback on the story, not the features.
4. If you set up a clear feedback process and teach your clients how to give great feedback, they will give you relevant and useful feedback.
5. If you make clear decisions about the feedback and communicate those decisions back to the client, they'll trust that you are listening to them.

With practice, these principles will become second nature. Not only will you feel a lot better about your presentation, but your team will collectively make a much better product.

ACKNOWLEDGMENTS

NATURALLY, I ASKED FOR feedback while writing this book. I used my own process, told people what I wanted to know about, and gave them clear instructions on how to get it to me. These fine people gave great (not always complimentary, but always useful) feedback and ultimately made the book a lot better: Charlie Lison, Chad Cogdill, Adam Polansky, Sally Bagshaw, Margaret L. Ruwoldt, Matt Fenwick, Josh Line, Justin Thor Hoyer, Claire Agnew, Mags Hanley, Feina You, Natasha Dwyer, Joshua Ogle, and Sarah Stokes. Thank you!

RESOURCES

IF YOU WANT TO dive deeper into presentation skills, or want to learn about how to present other types of work, here are some great books:

- *Banish your Inner Critic*, Denise Jacobs. This is an excellent read that will give you more confidence to stand in front of people, present your ideas, and know your ideas are good.
- *Communicating Design*, 2nd ed., Dan Brown. When I was learning to be a designer, I almost wore out Dan's first edition of this book. The second edition is, of course, just as good. It focuses on the different kinds of diagrams and reports we often present, so it will help a lot if you are still wondering *what* to present.
- *Communicating the User Experience: A Practical Guide for Creating Useful UX Documentation*, Richard Caddick and Steve Cable. This book is packed full of details about how to create UX deliverables. It's a great read for beginners.
- *Demystifying Public Speaking*, Lara Hogan. Lara provides clear, actionable advice on public speaking—whether you're speaking to a small group or a large group.
- *Design Is a Job* and *You're My Favorite Client*, Mike Monteiro. I group these two books not just because they are by Mike, but because you should read both of them. Together, they will help you work well with clients. It was at a workshop with Mike that I first heard anyone talk about *teaching* clients how to give feedback, and my presentations became better immediately after.

- *Designing for the Digital Age,* Kim Goodwin. Kim's book covers just about everything you'll need to know to design digital products. It's packed with practical details on the design process, interface design, and so much more. I mention it here, not only because it is great, but also because it's one of the few books I own that actually covers presenting design work.
- *Discussing Design: Improving Communication and Collaboration through Critique,* Adam Connor and Aaron Irizarry. This book covers how to present to your own team and colleagues. It is the perfect partner and will help you have better design discussions with other designers.

INDEX: PRESENTING DESIGN WORK

ABOUT THE AUTHOR

Donna Spencer is an independent design consultant with twenty-ish years of expertise across the entire design spectrum—from strategy to delivery and everything in between. She has solved a wide range of design problems across various industries, with a particular emphasis on information architecture and complex employee experience problems. Recognized internationally as a leading UX practitioner, Donna frequently presents her work at conferences and has written five UX-related books. She created UX Australia and ran it for nine years.

12

A BOOK APART

CULTIVATING CONTENT DESIGN

BETH DUNN

FOREWORD BY
ANN HANDLEY

BRIEFS

Publisher: Jeffrey Zeldman
Designer: Jason Santa Maria
Executive director: Katel LeDû
Managing editor: Lisa Maria Marquis
Editors: Sally Kerrigan, Chris Hagge, Caren Litherland
Book producer: Ron Bilodeau

ISBN: 978-1-952616-06-8

A Book Apart
New York, New York
http://abookapart.com

TABLE OF CONTENTS

For Minnie and Eva, my great-grandmother and great-aunt. Lifelong (and long-lived) readers, writers, teachers, and beacons of good cheer.

FOREWORD

HI, CONTENT FRIEND.

Beth invited me to write three-hundred words for this book foreword. That's an Instagram caption, really. At least for a writer like me, who always seeks to capture nuance and impart gravitas.

So just three-hundred words? Well, that doesn't seem quite enough to set the stage, especially for such an important book as this.

The pressure. She's on.

Let's hop to it. Just as Beth did when, a mere few paragraphs into this book, she articulates perfectly the tension so many of us feel as content strategists, producers, designers.

We love our jobs. We believe in content's ability to transform organizations. Yet we aren't seen as strategic partners. Too often we get the directive: "Just give me three-hundred words." Or: "Can you just make this sound better?"

No one scoots over to make room for us at the Table of Strategic Decision-Making; no one views as more than grammar geeks. (Also: Everyone qualifies an ask with "just." Annoying.)

As Beth puts it: "You're always frosting a really terrible cake, but you don't know how to get your hands on the recipe book—how to change the way content works in your organization."

So that's what Beth does here. And beautifully.

Beth doesn't just tell you about the tools you'll need (the cake pan, the mixing bowl, and the measurements, in this analogy). She gives you the power to fundamentally change your organization's approach to content. She gives you the recipe, the raw ingredients, and the entire kitchen, complete with a Viking range and hood (the 48-inch professional-series model).

Beth also offers tactical ideas to truly bake in (LOL) your position as a strategic content lead—giving you newfound respect, influence, esteem, reverence, support, appreciation, access...plus a squad of sous chefs and a finer crumb on your cake. And a tighter butt.

Just kidding on that last one. Maybe.

In my own work, I seek to empower content creators and strategists to do work that matters. You already do work that matters—so this is your opportunity to get your entire organization to understand your worth.

Now you can have your cake. And everyone else gets to eat it, too.

—Ann Handley

INTRODUCTION

THIS IS NOT A BOOK ABOUT how to do content design. It's not about how to write error messages, blog posts, website pages, or onboarding guides. It isn't even about how to do the research, discovery, and exploration necessary before all the writing begins.

You probably already know how to do all those wonderful things. And if you don't, or you need a refresher, there are some truly superb books, courses, and conferences out there that cover these topics in loving detail. You can check them out anytime—but please don't take them for granted. Not too long ago, you'd have been seriously hard-pressed to find high-quality resources that focused on content design as a fully fledged discipline. It wasn't that long ago that it was just as difficult to find other practitioners working on content design as their full-time job.

But in the past decade or so, all that has changed. Content design is *everywhere* now. It's a term people in very different disciplines throw around with abandon. And it has never been easier to learn the fundamentals of content design, content strategy, and user experience (UX) writing, or to find a job that requires these skills.

And yet.

Even now that we have a bookshelf full of books, now that we have content design courses we can take online or at a handful of accredited schools, now that we're surrounded and supported by a global community of like-minded friends, content designers still struggle to drive visible impact, influence strategy, and drill down to the real core of what content can do.

Some of this is perfectly fair, because the discipline is still an emerging one compared to other disciplines we often work alongside (UX design, engineering, or product management, for example). It's no wonder we sometimes feel that few people in our own organizations really know our true worth. Sometimes we're still figuring it out for ourselves.

But we're not *that* new. The value of content design isn't completely unknown, unproven, or unquantified. Let's be honest: content design has been around long enough, and has made enough of a difference to businesses, organizations, and users all over the world, that we should all feel we're standing on firm ground by now.

Do you feel like you're standing on firm ground?

You're not alone

The content people I talk to tell me they feel hampered by process and politics, by a dearth of respect, and by a chronic lack of investment and head count. They're often solo practitioners working in a sea of people who clearly want and need their help, yet don't consider them to be strategic partners. They say they're brought into projects too late to be of any but the most superficial assistance, and are rarely, if ever, given the chance to demonstrate clearly what they can do.

Does any of this sound familiar?

Here's what I'm guessing. I'm going to bet you're already really freaking good at your job. I bet you have incredible editorial, content-strategy, and content-design chops. And for the skills you still want or need to develop, you have the wherewithal to find the books, courses, and conferences that can help. (You can even start with the Resources section of this book.)

I'm also betting that you long for the chance to exercise some of those content chops even more—that what you really struggle with is the chance to do the work you know you can do, at the right stage of the game, with partners and stakeholders who know exactly the strategic value your presence brings.

You're tired of being pulled in at the eleventh hour to provide the "magic word" that will make a poorly planned product launch suddenly snap into sense, when the real problem is that no one clearly articulated the target audience for it eight or twelve months ago—when, as usual, you weren't in the room.

If that sounds like you, you know firsthand the pain of polishing content that has been built on a faulty foundation. It feels like you're always frosting a really terrible cake, but you don't know how to get your hands on the recipe book—how to change the way content works in your organization.

You might be thinking, *That's why we need to hire more writers and content designers for my team.* Or, *That's why we need to change our project management process, so I'll be involved in projects from the start.*

But I will firmly yet lovingly disagree. Because while these solutions might help in the short run, they won't really strike at the heart of the matter. If the teams you want to embed with don't know what content people can do, it won't do you much good to hire an army of writers. And, frankly, you're unlikely to get more people hired unless people at the higher levels of your organization have a real, bone-deep understanding of what it is people like you can do and how your work advances your company's real business needs.

People don't get a bone-deep understanding of something by hearing you say it for the hundredth time. They get it when you show them what the work looks like when it's done right, when you meet them where they are, and when you use the language, metaphors, and metrics that matter to them.

More than anything right now, what you need is some way to create the conditions in which you can do great content design. That's what I hope to provide in this book: a way for you to stretch your wings and really get a whack at the full suite of content work that I call *full-stack content design.*

Full-stack content design

Full-stack content design can only become a reality across your whole team when they've had a sort of content conversion experience—when something so radical has happened that they've changed their minds, their approach, their entire outlook on life. It's what some people might call a fundamental psychic change. And keep in mind you'll probably have to go through a shift in mindset yourself. This book is here to help you do all of that.

I know. That sounds like a lot for a relatively small book. But it does offer a path forward if you're stuck. It offers a way out of feeling like it's you against the world, like the deck is stacked against you, like content can't win. Because that mindset is probably getting you nowhere. And if this book gets you anywhere, it'll be somewhere better than that.

This book covers principles I worked out for myself long before I was even working in tech. Since then, I've worked with other content people in a variety of different settings, on different team sizes and types, helping them find their voice, express the voice of their company, and grow the impact a content practice can have on their organization's success.

Will this book apply to every content person, on every team, everywhere? Certainly not. It's likely to be most useful to folks working in-house on a fast-growing product, marketing, or services team. You might have to tweak it to your own purposes here and there. But regardless of your situation, it can work for you if you give it a try.

The change starts with you

Before you can change how other people see you, you're going to have to change how you see—and present—yourself. You know you're much more than just a proofreader and polisher of punctuation. You're a full-stack content designer, or you wouldn't have picked up this book.

You know that full-stack content design involves much more than just correcting grammatical errors or striking the right tone; after all, it does little good to correct Oxford commas if the ideas, format, structure, or delivery method aren't the right fit for the audience and their needs. That's why full-stack content design has to start with scoping out projects and deciding on goals; continue through research, testing, iteration, and change; and keep right on going through launch, publication, and continuous improvements.

But how do you get your hands on that kind of work?

What you need is to be working inside a full-stack content organization: one where every person on every team:

- sees the full content stack clearly,
- knows why it's important to the work *they* do,
- knows how to do some of it themselves to a baseline of proficiency, and
- knows when they're in trouble and need professional content help.

So the question really is this: How do you transform your organization into a full-stack content powerhouse?

It's a process, not an event

The process laid out in this book will help you change your organization from the inside out with love, empathy, and a deep concern for the things that matter most to the people you work with. Yes, you will find new ways to demonstrate how great content works and the value you offer. Better yet, you'll find new ways every day to drive real value in your company, and make a real difference in your coworkers' and customers' lives.

Because it's not about the silos that separate us in organizations. It's about how far we can go when we travel together.

Here's how it'll go:

- In Chapter 1, we'll explore how full-stack content design works. You'll get a clear picture of what it should look like, how you'll know if it's working, where it might need some help, and what you'll want to accomplish at each stage of the game.
- In Chapter 2, you'll learn how to spark a love of great content across your whole team, guide your colleagues to ask better content questions, and teach them how to use you as a strategic resource (instead of a human proofreading machine).
- In Chapter 3, we'll discuss how to design content workshops that speak meaningfully to your team's goals while opening hearts and minds to the real business impact of full-stack content work.

- In Chapter 4, you'll create a plan for prioritizing and championing great content at scale. You'll build on the strong culture you've created around content design, and you'll get more strategic about how you support others in their work.

The work does carry a risk of some intriguing side effects. Among other wonderful things, finding yourself within a full-stack content organization means you—and other content folk like you—will have the breathing room you need to be able to pick and choose where you can add the most value. It means you can step in and out of projects—or leave projects in others' capable hands—without needing to micromanage every little part of the content process yourself. You'll be focused on meaning, not minutia. And you'll have the power to be a real catalyst for change.

That change starts with you. It starts by changing your perception of the world you're operating in. It's not a world of us versus them, of people who love words and people who don't, of grammar fanatics and philistines. It's a world composed of people striving for an identical goal, curious about new ways to serve your customers as best you can. It's a world full of content champions, and content champions you just haven't activated yet.

This book is about how to ignite them—how to light them up from the inside with the power of content and create an organization that shines like a beacon of full-stack content design.

1

FULL-STACK CONTENT DESIGN

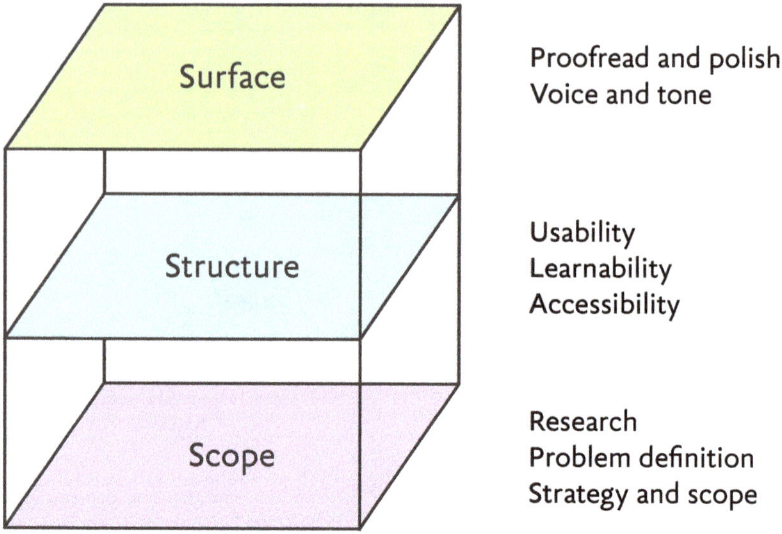

FIG 1: A full-stack content design organization invests in and supports the people and practices that contribute to each layer of the stack.

MAYBE YOU'VE SEEN PEOPLE in other fields refer to themselves as "full-stack" practitioners. What they mean is they're able to contribute to the success of a project at every stage of the work, beginning to end, front to back.

Full-stack marketers, for instance, can gather data, analyze results, design experiments, run tests, create a complete marketing strategy, and do the tactical work of executing it. Full-stack engineers cover a similar breadth: backend, frontend, security, performance, testing, quality assurance. From soup to nuts, they can do it all.

Full-stack content designers play a strong role at every stage of the game, too: research and brainstorming, determining strategy and scope, sketching out flows, testing for usability and accessibility, proofreading and polishing the final result, measuring success and iterating based on the results. Soup to nuts. You can do it all.

To illustrate this range of contributions, I've reimagined the classic "Layers of UX" popularized by designer Jesse James

Garrett (http://bkaprt.com/ccd12/01-01/, PDF). Full-stack content design has three layers: Scope, Structure, and Surface (**FIG 1**). Each layer involves different types of content work: from level-setting and discovery, to creative output, to polishing and perfecting, rinse and repeat.

That's what full-stack content design is. It's not really about different stages of a chronological process, or different components of a final user experience. It's about the practices and people involved in creating digital content. Power up those people, invest in those practices, and you empower your process.

So what does this full-stack content design look like in practice? Let's take a closer look at each layer in turn.

SCOPE

The first layer is the place where everything starts (or should start, at least). It's the part of the process where you explore the problem space, discover what's possible, home in on your approach, and plan for everything that comes next in the project.

A content designer might be involved with a number of different activities in the Scope layer, usually across three areas of focus: research, problem definition, and strategy and scope.

Research

Content designers often work alongside researchers and analysts to write questions and scripts; conduct interviews; and parse, analyze, and present the results. And since content designers tend to be highly attuned to language and meaning, we often pick up on words, phrases, and cognitive pathways that others might miss. We hear it when users insist on a certain metaphor to describe what they're trying to do, and can craft interface copy that will match their mental model.

Working in partnership with researchers can be magical. The researchers I've worked with have often been delighted by the fresh perspectives a content person can bring to their work.

Finding one or two researchers who love working with you can be a great start to establishing a full-stack content practice.

Problem definition

Out of research comes the work of problem definition: working alongside product managers to articulate the problem the team is trying to solve. While the product manager often has a clear vision for this, a content designer can memorably capture it in the form of a written story, loosely illustrated storyboard, or user journey map.

Many teams start out trying to solve a different problem than the one that actually emerges from their research. That's not meant as a criticism—it's part of the process. You start in one place, do some research, and then refine your approach. That's why it's important to get very good at articulating the problem as you see it from the start, so you know just what it is you're refining as the research results start to roll in. Content designers help write the story of the problem, and then rewrite it over time.

There are many different ways a team might create a shared story to describe the core problem, such as a user journey map, a long-form narrative story, an illustrated storyboard, or a set of cartoons. They're all slightly different ways of pulling data points and details into one clear and compelling narrative arc for you and your team to rally around.

Clear and crisp problem definition is particularly important when you're working on a product with a broad and deep footprint, with teams that value rapid iteration and experimentation, or when coordinating work across multiple independent, autonomous teams on different pieces of the same cross-product user flow. Without clear problem definition, you might end up with different teams taking different stabs at the same problem; but with it, you retain small-team autonomy while keeping your goals and efforts aligned. Crafting a compelling story is also key for getting buy-in from leaders or stakeholders to move ahead with the project.

Strategy and scope

Part of the process of problem definition is deciding where to draw boundaries around your efforts. By corralling the project's purview and explicitly leaving aside what you won't be trying to solve, you can help your team avoid scope creep and stay focused.

Deciding on the scope of the project is in itself a strategic move. You're deciding that *this*, not *that*, is the challenge you're going to solve. A content designer can help a team make this decision clearly, and document it in a way that's easy for them to remember and share. A well-articulated scope, along with clear project definition, will help determine the strategic moves this project demands.

STRUCTURE

The Structure layer is where you start working on the organization, categorization, and hierarchy of ideas. It's where you begin designing your content to best meet users where they are without overwhelming, distracting, immobilizing, or annoying them.

Content designers will work with their team—often a mix of designers, engineers, information architects, and others—to present the solution to the problem with a focus on usability, learnability, and accessibility. These three areas often overlap, because they are mutually reinforcing, interwoven, and really inseparable at heart.

Usability

Usable content is designed with a careful eye toward how much cognitive load each step or stage carries, and creates consistency across the experience with the patterns the user has experienced elsewhere (in your product or in similar experiences in their life). Usable content makes sense to the user in the context of their own world.

This means your content uses metaphors, symbols, and language that already resonate with your audience. Usable content is inclusive content—you don't use words or elements that would only be comprehensible or welcoming to someone from a certain background, religion, gender, or class.

Learnability

Learnable content carefully considers which concepts might require explanation, clarification, or active practice to learn, and how to offer users the chance to learn them. The sequence, weighting, separation, combination, and organization of ideas, objects, actions, and assets are all factors in learnable content.

- It's important to consider what other experiences are already in the product (or are being worked on right now) and how those experiences might interact with or affect the experience at hand. As the resident content practitioner, you're likely to have a more holistic view of how different angles of the user experience come together across the whole product; the Structure layer is the best time to contribute that perspective.
- On a finer scale, you want to make sure the language and images you're planning to use match up with what's used elsewhere in the product. What metaphors or mental models are at play at other points in the experience? How might those metaphors extend to this project? How might they break down?
- It's often useful at this stage to assemble a simple inventory of the nouns (objects) and verbs (actions) most often used throughout the experience that are relevant to this project. Rather than undertake a full content audit, you might just gather a list of the objects and actions you're dealing with here. How do they fit (or not fit) the story you're trying to tell?

Accessibility

Your content won't be usable or learnable if it's not accessible, too. Designing your content for accessibility first will make it more inclusive, regardless of user circumstance, ability, or need.

Font size, color contrast, plain language, adaptability to screen readers, and much more all go into designing accessible content. Words need to be readable, in the sense that the user needs to be able to see and read the letters on the screen; and the text needs to be written at a reading level that optimizes comprehension. Text written at a sixth- or seventh-grade reading level is generally the most easily understood by all users, regardless of education level, industry, or background. Use the Resources section at the end of this book to learn more about who needs accessible content (spoiler alert: it's everyone) and how to write, structure, and design it.

You may come across people who resist your efforts to keep content at an accessible reading level. They may say you're "dumbing it down" or something equally offensive. You can tell them from me that the only thing that's "dumbed down" about accessible content is having an outdated, narrow, closed-minded idea of what "accessible" means.

Test early, test often

A common mistake at this stage is to get too invested in the words and images you're using to organize your design. Teams and individuals can easily latch on to words, images, naming conventions, and mental models that make more sense to them than to the user, which is why it's important to keep on testing and iterating with real users throughout the life of a project.

At this point, remember that your content is provisional, even placeholder content. Think of it as "low-fidelity" content you will refine over time. Some teams make it a practice to keep the images in early designs deliberately sketchy, unfinished, or at a low resolution, and to set the text in Comic Sans or something equally off-brand as a visual reminder that the content is provisional and subject to change.

SURFACE

The final Surface layer is where the content is refined and finalized. You already know which concepts and ideas are most important, and when and how they should be encountered and met. Content designers usually work alongside designers, marketers, support reps, and salespeople to make sure the experience they've designed aligns with the house style guide; fits into the larger user narrative arc; and is as easy as possible to understand, market, demo, sell, and support.

Proofread and polish

This is where UX writing and illustration come to the fore. You've been creating and testing low-fidelity content as part of the content design process so far. Now it's time to finalize your verbal, visual, and structural choices, and make them consistent with your house style in terms of spelling, grammar, punctuation, and form.

It's helpful at this stage to refer to some of your earlier work to inventory the words, images, and metaphors used across the rest of the product or experience to ensure your final product is consistent with them. If you've introduced any new terminology, concepts, or conventions, now's a good time to add them to your style guide and other internal glossaries or tools.

Voice and tone

It's also a good time to inspect your content for any voice or tone wrinkles, and to smooth them right out. Ensure that your words, images, and ideas are consistent with your brand voice, and that you're using the right tone for the situation at hand.

I like to think of *voice* as defining who you are—you're always you—while *tone* is how you behave in different situations. For example, I might define my own voice as friendly, helpful, quirky, and kind—but I'll present those aspects of my personality in different (and hopefully appropriate) ways, depending on whom I'm speaking to (my mother, my best friend, or the Queen of England) and the context of our conversation (a phone call, a dinner party, or getting a life peerage conferred).

You might notice that these late-stage activities on the Surface are the ones many people outside the content community tend to think we spend most (if not all) of our time on. But when you've been present and active at each stage of the game, the people you work with will have seen with their own eyes how important a role content plays from beginning to end.

START WHERE YOU ARE

You may feel you're stuck at the top of the stack, focused primarily on the Surface layer of content work. If you're on a product team, that means you're mostly spending your time on interface word choice and making minor adjustments to voice and tone. If you do marketing, tech writing, or internal communications, it might be more about copywriting, editing, and proofreading for house style. It's important work, and we tend to excel at it.

The first step in the full-stack mindset shift is accepting the reality of the top of the stack. While your natural impulse may be to bang on pots and pans and fight for a seat at the table farther down the stack, it's often more effective to start where you're already having an impact—right in the Surface layer.

It sounds counterintuitive, but hear me out. If you're stuck in an endless loop of proofreading and polish, start with the people you work with on that: designers, marketers, salespeople. They already know and trust you. You have a foundation of credit with them. These folks are likely to be your first converts—the content champions you'll enlist on your team.

Why not start by training these enchanting people to do some of this Surface work for themselves? Not all of it, naturally. But surely you can entrust some of the proofreading and polish to a group of enthusiastic trainees.

Moving a little Surface work off of your plate frees you up to go deeper into the stack. If you're currently buried in work at the top of the stack, and you *don't* enlist others' help, you'll never get that chance. And if nobody gets to see the deeper work you can do, they won't think to ask it of you in the future. It's a vicious cycle.

Hoarding your work also runs the risk of leaving talented people untapped. Literally every team I've ever worked with has had a handful of content enthusiasts lurking just under the surface, if you just give them a scratch. If you encourage and empower them even a little, these hidden content champions will surprise you with what they can do.

The goal isn't to never do Surface work again. It's to give yourself options. When you equip other people to do this work, too, you give yourself the gift of choice. You can choose to let them do it, or you can jump in and help out. There will always be lots of Surface work to be done, so you'll never stop the cycle if you don't find a way to let some of it go.

The downside is that you will no longer be the lone, magical wordsmith who works wonders behind closed doors. Sharing your skillset may erode some of the mystical glow around content design. And that's not a bad thing.

Because then you'll be free to rebrand yourself from magical wordsmith to problem definer, scope and strategy wrangler, accessibility advocate, and so much more. It's a simple question of bandwidth and branding.

STRIKE UP THE BAND

I'll say it again: you'll never get the chance to do the deeper stack work if you're swamped with Surface work that only *you* can get done. And if that's the only type of work people ever see you do, that's all that people will ever think you can do.

That's why the next step in this process is to help the people you work with recognize what good content looks like, understand the value of great content *to them in their roles*, and learn how to do at least some of that work for themselves.

And the way we do that is by getting everybody to sing the same song.

2

SING OUT LOUD

I ONCE WORKED WITH A GUY who was the king of earworms. Every once in a while, he'd try to see how long it would take him to get the whole office humming the same tune. He'd either walk down the hallway a few times, humming a few bars, or maybe he'd just scrawl a few potent lyrics on the whiteboard in a few conference rooms.

That's all it took, usually. And before lunchtime, we were all tapping our feet to the same jaunty beat.

We all have the power to drive change like that. The trick is to decide what song it is you want to put in people's heads, and then find a way to get it out into the world.

THE STYLE GUIDE TRAP

Content folk will often turn to their style guide to try to get people in their organization all singing the same tune. Usually when a company gets around to creating a house style guide, it's because they've discovered they have too many different people creating too much disparate content, and they want it to sound more like they're all singing the same song. Style guides are widely considered to be great tools for getting your team to start doing just that.

So why do we have such a hard time getting people to use them?

Maybe you've already noticed that the only people who actually read and use most style guides are the people who created them in the first place. Yeah, it's really just us. No matter how many times we urge other people to check the style guide, most of them don't.

And I truly don't blame them. The fact of the matter is that most people don't like or even understand style guides—what's in them, how to use them, why they even exist. Telling people to "use the style guide" is a bit like telling me I should keep a scientific calculator next to me at all times. Even if I were to follow such bizarre advice, I wouldn't know what to use it for, or even how. Honestly, its very presence would stress me out.

This is how most people feel when we remind them there are "writing rules" they need to follow. To most people, these rules are strange, oppressive, arbitrary, and unclear. The very fact that they exist at all stresses them out.

That's why, when we present ourselves as the Keepers of the Writing Rules, we tend not to get invited to things. We're a constant, visceral reminder that there are rules to this whole content situation, and that most people are probably breaking twenty of them at a time. Nobody likes having that person at their party, or meeting, or brainstorming session—that person is, frankly, a drag. Most people aren't at all sure what we'd have to offer besides sitting there and correcting everyone's grammar at will, which is a downer—and not even helpful most of the time.

So a major step in gaining control of our destiny has to be finding a different way of getting people to sing along with our song. And that means we need to learn to let go of our beloved style guides.

NOBODY CARES ABOUT YOUR STYLE GUIDE

Style guides are not teaching tools. They're sets of rules. People don't like to follow rules, because rules are not fun. But you know what's extremely fun? Writing great content. The trouble is, most people don't see the connection between the rules and the content.

Teaching other people to learn and apply the rules of writing is like insisting people learn to read musical notation instead of just helping them burst into song. You might know that it's key to making a strong composition, but they're pretty sure they'd rather skip right to singing a rock anthem at the top of their lungs.

They're not wrong. That's how people learn to love, support, and even make fantastic music themselves. You have to love it so much you can't help dancing along. Do you know how many great musicians never learned to read music? Let's start with Eddie Van Halen, Dave Grohl, Paul McCartney, Jimi Hendrix—shall I go on?

You need to find a creative way to get folks to sing along. The key is to find some lovable way to regularly get your song in front of them, all of the time. Whatever you can do routinely and do well—use that as a vehicle for your catchy style-guide tune. Some possibilities:

- **Posters.** Create a bunch of memorable posters for your office with visuals and text that show people what your voice and tone look like in action.
- **Wallpaper.** Create a series of delightful Zoom backgrounds for your distributed team. Replenish the supply often, so they never get stale.
- **Internal newsletters.** Never underestimate the power of an email newsletter, especially one that includes pictures of your adorable coworkers, their children, and their pets.
- **Blog posts.** Write about life at your company, profile some of your best customers, interview members of the leadership team.
- **Instagram posts.** Offer a peek into a day-in-the-life of a new employee, a user, the beloved barista who works down the street.
- **Curated playlists.** Use the power of music to quite literally get your team singing the same song.

If you look hard enough, you'll find a format that works for you, your goal, and your company, too. Do something different, something that doesn't exist today, for your team. If your company tends to wallow in words, use photography or illustrations to grab their attention and make them look up. If your company already has an internal newsletter or playlist, just start your own.

(And remember: you don't have to ask permission to start humming in the hallways. Often the unofficial, underground, guerrilla marketing methods are best.)

It all depends on where your strengths lie, and what your organization will respond to. Just do whatever you think will work best in your world. I used to joke that the right batch of temporary tattoos could do the job, and I stand by that. Content is content. Come on. You're good at this stuff.

And that's the key, really. It has to be good. It has to be something people *want* to tune in to. They need to enjoy—love—it, want to sing it out loud in their car. Remember, this is meant to be their content rock ballad. Make them want to turn it up to eleven.

RAISE YOUR VOICE

When you start creating this catchy content, stay away from telling people *about* the rules at all—at this stage of things, at least. *Don't even make this content about content.* Whatever vehicle you choose to get your message across, use it as a means to show good content in action, not to dissect *how* it was made. You're trying to build a karaoke machine, not instruct the masses in musical theory. Make it look easy. Make it look *fun.*

I like to use an internal newsletter as my karaoke machine. But that's just because (1) I love writing newsletters, and (2) I have the honor of writing one at my company. It's called the WIN, which stands for Weekly Internal Newsletter, which is just what it is. Among other things, it's meant to be a lovable earworm that promotes our fantastic culture—who we are and what we believe, honor, and support—which extends to our company voice and tone.

The WIN is simple and streamlined, lighthearted and fun. *Because our house style is to create content that's simple and streamlined, lighthearted and fun.* That's the song I want to get into everyone's head.

Maybe your house style isn't lighthearted and fun. Maybe your challenge instead is to get your organization to create clear, unbiased content without a glimmer of spark. That's okay, too. You can demonstrate how clear, unbiased content doesn't need to be boring (and, in fact, shouldn't be—content can't be clear if you've put your audience to sleep).

Maybe your company is already drowning in internal newsletters. That's okay, too. Create content that those newsletters will want to include. Interview some employees. Profile some customers. Find a way to tell a story people will want to hear, and do it in a way that shows your house style in action. I do love an internal newsletter, and I put it to you that even if you have loads of them already, it's quite possible yours will leave them all in the dust. So don't knock it till you try it, is all I suggest.

It doesn't even need to be that much of a lift. Here's how it works for my newsletter:

1. Every Wednesday, I send out a quick reminder that everyone is invited to submit to the WIN. This is usually just a fun illustration that matches the season, or something positive and unifying going on in the world, like reminding everyone that they love rescue puppies, or springtime.
2. Other people in the company will respond with a link to something they wrote that they want to promote—usually something that's just gone live on the company wiki. I don't know about your company, but we live and breathe on our internal wiki. (If it's not on the wiki, it didn't happen.) So if somebody wants to make sure the thing they wrote on the wiki has a fighting chance of getting seen by everyone at the company, they send it in to the WIN.
3. I add the link to the WIN—I've imposed a fairly arbitrary limit of just nine items, tops—with some zippy copy to promote it.

This last step is the key ingredient of the WIN, often forgotten when people start their own internal newsletters: I don't write any of the content that gets linked in the WIN. It's purely an act of curation on my part. This radically trims down the amount of time I have to spend on it, and makes it much more a snapshot of the company at that moment in time. It's not about me—it's about the people around me. All I do is write the copy that entices readers to click through to the submitted wiki post. That's it.

But that's everything. Because, honestly, most people *don't* click through. They just read my zippy copy. And that's okay, too, because that copy is written relentlessly in our house style, voice, and tone. It's brief, lighthearted, inclusive, optimistic, and fun. People read it, they get it, they internalize it over time.

And eventually, they realize that it has something they want.

WHAT A HERO WANTS

Remember: everybody at your company is a hero in their own story, too. And as we already know from crafting narratives, every hero has to want something.

What they want might not be to sound more like you (although they might say that when they email you after enjoying your catchy content for a few weeks or months). What they want is to reach that goal they have in their head. Hit their monthly sales target. Attract more great leads. Connect with customers more clearly. Win some executive buy-in. Writing in the voice and tone you've demonstrated is just a means to an end.

And what happens next, which absolutely will follow like night follows day, is that people very much want their content to sound more like that voice. They can't put their finger on it, but they know their content doesn't quite have that hook. And they want it to.

1. Does that sound too good to be true? I've seen it happen in all kinds of organizations, on all kinds of teams, in a wide variety of industries with different needs. I've seen it work for the dozens of people I've coached through the process.
2. We tend to forget—or at least grossly underestimate—that content created by someone who knows what they're doing will stand out from the crowd. When a talented writer puts strong content in front of people who need it, those people will take notice. And they will want to learn how to capture those skills for themselves.

HAVE FUN STORMING THE CASTLE

Instead of hammering at the rules, you built an attractive Trojan horse for your style, voice, and tone. Now you're quietly tiptoeing into everyone's inbox (or whatever) and getting them to sing along to something they actually enjoy, all while you slowly, stealthily get your brand voice and, yes, even style rules stuck in their head. As long as it's content they want to consume, they will start to internalize it, mimic it, and embrace it, *en masse*.

And that's exactly what you wanted to happen when you started this whole thing. It's all going according to plan.

3

WORKSHOPS THAT WORK

STOP ME IF YOU'VE HEARD THIS ONE: Somebody on the sales team wants you to look over the standard email they send to their best leads, to make it sound more human and friendly. Someone on the marketing team asks you for feedback on a landing page format that just isn't converting the way they think it should. Someone on the legal team wants to know how to make their dry and dusty terms of service sound less like legalese.

If you're a solo content person, or even part of a very small content team, you're probably quite used to these casual requests for editorial help. They always "should only take a minute," and, usually, they do. But those minutes pile up, don't they?

Now that you've been humming a catchy content tune all over the place, people are going to be asking you for help more than ever before. You might find these cries for help flattering, even fun to work on, but they may also be a source of additional stress on your workload. So why am I suggesting you generate even more?

Because you're going to start using these requests to grow your organization's content chops. From now on, when people ask you for tips, you're going to give them something even better than that.

You're going to suggest that you offer your best tips and tricks in the form of a *workshop for their whole team*.

I LIKE THE WAY YOU WORKSHOP

You might be surprised by how many people will think a workshop is a fantastic idea, so don't be shy about suggesting it. You're an expert they respected enough to ask for advice, and they'll be grateful for your time, energy, and support. They asked for your help because they think you're good at this stuff. And when you tell them to bring along their whole team, it means you're willing to share that knowledge with more people, which will make their jobs easier, too.

Running content workshops for teams that ask for your help will allow you to scale what you do like nothing else. But you're likely not already in the habit of running these kinds of workshops. You may be very well versed in the kind of workshop that tends to happen on design and UX teams, full of Post-it notes and ideation sprints and maybe the occasional improv game. I love improv games. But this isn't going to be that kind of workshop.

You're going to develop a very particular style of workshop—one designed to help teams tackle, for themselves, some vital component of your full-stack content practice.

No matter which layer of the content stack your hypothetical team needs help with, your workshop will follow the same five basic steps:

1. Do your research.
2. Diagnose the problem.
3. Find your five.
4. Terrible-ize it.
5. Teach your team.

The first four steps here are preparatory and will help you structure the format and content of the workshop itself, tailoring the message to what each team needs to hear most. The final stage, the workshop itself, is about an hour in length. Let's go through each step in turn.

DO YOUR RESEARCH

Start where any project starts: with basic research. In order to diagnose the problem this team needs help with, work with your contact person on the team—the one who originally asked you for help—to define:

1. the *container* for the content in question;
2. the *content* itself, also known as the message; and
3. the *goal* of the content, which you'll measure with an agreed-upon metric.

This part of the process is vital, so make sure to give yourself enough time to gather your notes and customize your workshop to the problem at hand. Your goal here is to deliver a workshop that opens this team's eyes to the full suite of content design as it applies to their jobs, so it's well worth the time it takes to fully prepare.

The container

Your first source document will be the original piece of content your contact brought to your attention. Ask yourself: What's the nature of the content they want help with? For example:

- A product team wants to write error messages that will reduce support calls.
- A sales team wants to create an email that will help them book demos.
- A marketing team wants to build a higher-converting landing page.

Error messages, emails, landing pages—these are all *containers* for the content you'll be working on. They're the delivery vehicles for the team's messaging.

It's possible that the container they're using isn't the right one for the message and goal, and that's something you might encourage the team to question during the workshop. It's a major teachable moment when you can get a team to see that in order to achieve the goal they have for this content, they might need to go deeper than adjusting the subject line or tone. But for now, the important thing is to help them see that there's a distinction between the content and the container, and that they can make choices about each.

The content

Next, identify the meaning of the *content* within that container. What's the message they're trying to get across? For example:

- The error message should tell the user what's wrong and what they can do next.
- The sales email should tell the user there's a solution to their problem.
- The landing page should convince the user that attending a webinar will answer their questions.

You'll often find that a piece of content is primarily concerned with getting the user to understand something new, or in a new way. It should also offer the user an action they can take as result, which is tied to the content's goal.

The goal

Now that you know what the content is and what it's trying to communicate, you can identify its *goal*—the action taken by the user—and how the team measures the success of that goal. For example:

- The product team wants users to return to the login screen and try logging in again, measured by the number of users who successfully log in after getting this error.
- The sales team wants their email recipients to book a live demo, measured by the number of demos booked every month through that email's link.
- The marketing team wants people to reserve a spot in their webinar, measured by the number of people who register using that landing page's link.

Defining the metric is a key part of planning the content workshop, since it allows you to clearly and explicitly tie what you teach them to the metrics that govern the world they live in. You've got to gear the whole thing around the metrics that matter to them.

Make sure the metric is clearly measurable and has real business value to the team. It should be a metric that keeps them up at night, one that makes a regular appearance on their monthly meeting slides or performance reviews.

Ask them for the actual baseline number for this metric that they're hitting right now. Then ask them to tell you what a good outcome would be. What *should* that number look like? That's your shared goal. You are now all on the same team, clearly, explicitly, trying to achieve the same ends.

DIAGNOSE THE PROBLEM

Once you've compiled all this research—what type of container you're dealing with, what the content is supposed to make the reader think or do, and how to know if it's working—verify your conclusions with your team contact. It's important that you go into this workshop speaking the team's language—that the way *you* think about the container, content, and goal is perfectly aligned with how *they* think about them.

Ask your contact to gather different examples of the same type of content from other folks on the team. You don't need a million of them—about five or six will do nicely. You just want to get a representative sample of what they're using today.

Once you have these in hand, read through them slowly. Resist the urge to edit them as you go along. That urge will be strong. All you're really doing at this point is trying to decide where the team needs the most help: at the Surface layer, the Structure layer, or the Scope layer.

Surface challenges

Content that has challenges primarily at the Surface layer will be rife with errors of style, voice, and tone—but that's all that's really wrong with it. Ask yourself: If you fixed all of the grammatical errors, bad sentence formation, misjudgments of your brand voice, or tone misalignments, would it be fine? Or are there deeper, more serious problems lurking beneath? Can this content be saved purely by giving more attention to the process of proofreading and polishing? Or does the problem extend beyond that, into the content structure itself?

Structure challenges

Structure problems are a bit harder to diagnose, especially if there are also a lot of Surface issues to distract your eye. Ignore those for now, and look closely at the content's information order, hierarchy, usability, and accessibility. Are the sentences, paragraphs, menu options, or flow in the right order, or do they need a complete overhaul? Is the meaning clear? If you corrected all the Surface problems, would it still be a mess?

There is some potential overlap here with Surface issues, of course, especially when it comes to diagnosing problems related to usability, learnability, and accessibility. Many companies consider it an issue of house style to choose shorter words, avoid jargon, and use plain language—all core usability considerations. But questions of usability tend to raise deeper issues than just changing one word out for another. Adjusting the reading level of a whole document usually requires a more wholesale approach, often rethinking the structure and scope of the document. So while I agree in principle that content usability can and should be addressed in a style guide, I find that solutions to these issues typically require a much deeper dive than pure Surface problems do.

Scope challenges

Content with problems at the Scope layer tends to be unclear on what that user's next step might be, or—more often—offers too many possible next steps to pursue. *Either call your senator or write them or donate or email us for more details.* That's a serious muddle. It's content that is trying to do too much at once.

I'd argue that "one" is the right number for suggested next steps (also known as the *call to action,* or CTA) in any given piece of content. (Maybe two, if you count the option of "No, thanks.") Content should convince you to book a demo now—or don't. Update your account info now—or don't. Call your senator—or assume somebody else will do it for you. Those are your options. Do or do not. There is no try.

If you suspect you're dealing with problems at the Scope layer, revisit your notes about the content's goal. Is the action getting diluted by a lot of *ifs, ands,* or *buts*? If so, go back to your contact person and ask them to clarify the content's goal. What's the *one* action they want the reader to take?

Watch out if the answer is something like "be aware." We generally write content to convince users to *do* something. Sometimes that involves an intermediary step of learning or gaining awareness. But the next step is almost always, "So now do this thing." If that isn't clear in the content, you know to focus on Scope discussions in your workshop.

Once you've diagnosed the problem and determined whether the greatest need is to address the Surface, Structure, or Scope of the content, it's time to move on to the next step.

FINDING YOUR FIVE

Say you've gotten a nice, representative handful of emails from a sales team—samples of the emails they send to prospects who might want to book a demo or contact a sales rep. They don't know what, exactly, is wrong with the emails, but they know they're not working as well as they should. And since they've tried everything else—sending them more often, less often, earlier and later in the day or on different days of the week, and so on—they reckon it has to do with the content itself.

At first glance, you can spot Surface problems. They have a bunch of minor bad habits that, taken together, are keeping their readers from getting on board with the whole demo idea. The order, flow, and amount of information looks fine, and they're not trying to do too much or too little with this one piece of content, either. There's a single, clearly stated CTA at the end. Okay. This baby needs some proofreading and polishing help.

You take a closer look still. Like a lot of people these days, these content creators tend to rely on commas and run-on sentences to establish a breezy, conversational tone. For instance, one of the sample emails starts out:

Hey [name]!

Thanks so much for visiting our site the other day, hope you found what you needed!

You jot down something about overusing exclamation marks and comma splices, and sip your tea for a second or two while you ponder whether "Hey" or "Hi" would be the most appropriate greeting in an email like this. You double-check your source material and, sure enough, this team is focused on reaching people in the US, mostly in entry-level roles, in a fairly casual industry, where a lighthearted voice is desired. So kicking things off with a low-key, casual "Hey" is probably just the ticket. So that's okay.

You notice the content creators have a tendency to say "our software" and "our site" more than they talk about "your needs" and "your team,' so you'll want to talk to them about who pronouns say is really the hero around here.

They might lean a bit too hard on needlessly longer words when a shorter word will do, like saying "utilize" instead of "use," or "leverage" instead of *literally any other word at all.* Also, there's an "incentivize" in there. Ew. Okay, you'll make sure to talk about plain language and short words.

You keep going, working your way through your documents until you've found five things you want this team to work on. Five things—that's all.

Keep it simple

You're not trying to compile a list of every mistake they make—you're looking for the top five issues that, if addressed in a uniform way, would significantly raise the effectiveness of their work.

Any more than five things and you run a real risk of overwhelming them. The message you want them to walk away with isn't, "Wow, content is super complex and hard," or "Gosh, I've been doing content so incredibly wrong." It's, "I can do this! I just need to do these five simple things." The confidence you give them in this workshop is just as important as the guidance you impart.

You know that there's a lot more to this than just five simple rules. But you also know that if they just did these five things differently, every single time, they'd see a difference in the content and in how well it does the job they're asking it to do.

Along with your five simple rules, you'll also show them the tools and resources available to help them, most of which, I promise you, they don't yet know exist. Or they might have heard of them (rumors of a style guide, whispers of voice-and-tone guidelines carried on the wind), but they don't really have any sense of why they might want to access them. Now they'll understand what those resources can do in the context of their own work.

Try to keep the workshop focused on just one content layer: Surface, Structure, or Scope. There's usually plenty to keep you occupied within just that one realm, and a tightly focused workshop will yield far better results.

By the end of this workshop, they'll be adept at navigating a layer of the stack as it applies to their content (which matters a great deal to them), and they'll see how investing in that layer will help them reach their team goals.

TERRIBLE-IZE IT

Now comes the best part: creating a composite version of the content that is absolutely *the worst.*

Take your team's sample content and wildly exaggerate the worst traits you've identified. If they're abusers of exclamation marks, put these everywhere. Comma splice fanatics? Leave no sentence unspliced. Push the needle on whatever five things you've decided to focus on and turn the awfulness all the way up to eleven. Make it really, *really* smelly and bad.

This accomplishes two important things: First, it makes the sample content you're going to ask them to work on at the end of the workshop so unrecognizable that no one on the team will feel bad or singled out. It'll be recognizable as the kind of content they need help with, but comfortably terrible enough that they know they're at least better than *that.*

Second, editing content that has been expertly terrible-ized is a surprisingly effective way of getting people to remember the rules you're teaching them. Subtlety isn't memorable; over-the-top, laugh-out-loud, cringeworthy content is.

And third (I know I said two things but I'm a writer, not a mathematician): terrible-izing content is fun. It's fun for you to do before the workshop—you will giggle a lot—and it's fun for the team when you give it to them to fix.

Remember the sage words of one of my dearest friends, who likes to remind me that "the second most powerful human urge is editing other people's writing."

The first most powerful urge, of course, is overusing exclamation marks. You can look it up.

TEACH YOUR TEAM

These workshops should never be more than an hour in length (again, you don't want to overwhelm people). The bulk of the time will be spent exploring the nature of the problem this team needs to solve, with about fifteen minutes at the end to work on the terrible-ized content.

Kick things off with an introduction to the layers of content design—Scope, Structure, and Surface—using something like the diagram found in this book. Give participants an overview of the work required to create quality content at each layer.

I find it helpful to ask them for a parallel in their own line of work. For instance, sales people often spend hours on research and planning before they get on a call, customizing their strategy and script to each potential customer—this can be a form of full-stack content design, too. Make them see that they're already content designers themselves, and that you're here to help them develop that muscle to hit their goals.

Spend the majority of your time going over the five principles you identified as being most relevant to this team. Don't go out of your way to make it clear that this is based on the work they provided you at the start. The more accidental it appears, the more likely it is they will see you as a trove of relevant, useful information that will help them move the metrics that matter most to their team. Walk them through any documentation, resources, playbooks, or guidelines that you have in your content arsenal, and point out areas of potential interest to them.

For instance, if a team needs help with basic style and tone, I'll spend a lot of time on those areas (and less time on, say, usability recommendations). Did they know we have guidance on how to use exclamation marks? Turns out, we do! They will write down this fact. It will probably be news to them. And they will be delighted to hear it. Remember, most people are swimming around in murky, eel-infested waters when it comes to writing content; they are generally grateful if you can throw them a rope and lead them safely to shore.

If you don't have playbooks and guidelines for each case you encounter, that's okay. Designing these workshops can serve as your own discovery research, informing you about the needs of your users (the internal teams at your company) and the resources that will help them do their jobs. If your first few workshops seem to center on questions of voice and tone, that's a great excuse to spend some time either creating or refining the guidance you have.

As time goes on, you'll probably find that the workshops start naturally going deeper down the layers. You don't need to have playbooks and libraries of guidance on hand when you start doing this work. The work will inform what you need to create. All you need to do is stay one chapter—sometimes even one page—ahead of the people you're working with and trying to help.

BE THE GUIDE, NOT THE GURU

Before long, you'll be regularly running these workshops—introducing teams to the idea of full-stack content design, showing off the finer points of whatever documentation will help them, and concentrating on five basic principles that can change the way they work.

In return, your colleagues will start to see the pursuit of quality content as the treasure they seek. And they'll know that the resources you're offering them are the map for that quest.

You might be uncomfortable with this, at first, if you're very secure in your role as the Keeper of the Words in your organization. But the more you shift how you see yourself—and how you're willing to be seen—the more you'll be able to empower the people around you. You're a fellow traveler who has been down these roads before, and you're ready to help your teammates successfully find their way through the content stack, too.

4

CONTENT AT SCALE

ONE OF THE MOST STARTLING effects of this process occurs when it all starts to work. One day you will wake up to an embarrassment of riches. You'll have multiple requests for content help, and it will *all* be of the kind you've been wanting to do. High-level, early-stage, strategic work. Full-on structural overhauling and rebuilding of an existing system or service. Gloriously engaging voice-and-tone work for a flow that serves a key user need.

Once you show people what you can do—and clearly demonstrate to them how it impacts the success metrics they care most about—the floodgates will open, and you'll suddenly have way too much work.

Wait. What? Wasn't this book supposed to help you *scale* what you do? Become more efficient, more selective, and *not* spread so thin?

Yes, and it absolutely will do all of that. But once you reach this inflection point—where you've officially teetered over from not-enough-of-the-right-kind of work to wanting to hide on a small island somewhere with an unlisted number—you've got a totally different problem on your hot little hands.

It's at this point that I would urge you *not* to start arguing for headcount. I know, I know, I'm such a buzzkill. But this is probably the most delicate stage of the proceedings, and it's so important that you don't rush. You're the one who promised you could do all this great work—so, at least for a while, you're the one who has to deliver the goods.

Now you need to get serious about how you'll prioritize the work.

PICKING YOUR PRIORITIZATION PLAN

The great news is there's no lack of handily acronymed prioritization protocols out there. You can take your pick. It's possible your team already uses something to prioritize their projects, but you might find it wasn't designed with full-stack content work in mind.

Don't be shy about developing your own approach to prioritizing your work. Remember, you're in charge of your own story. You get to decide if the narrative is "I have too much work" or "I have so many valid requests for work that I triage and support them in several different, equally effective and appropriate ways." I know which story I'd rather be in. But, hey, you do you.

For my money, any prioritization system that gives you a clean, numerical score is a workable plan. You may be quantifying highly subjective information, but you're not just conjuring numbers out of thin air; ideally, you're developing them in consultation with the stakeholders who want your help with something.

Start with a full and frank exchange of views with your stakeholders. How do they prioritize their own work today? If they already use a clear prioritization plan, see if you can extend it to the work you do. What considerations do they weigh when prioritizing projects? It might be a combination of things like how many users this project will impact, to what extent, how much effort and time it will take, and what the payoff will be. Maybe they already weigh considerations like these, and you can work together to figure out where this project falls on each sliding scale.

Maybe they go more on gut feel, or whichever project has the loudest voice arguing for it. Hey, it happens. That might be a great opportunity to gently suggest factoring in more quantifiable aspects, too. The important thing is that you work alongside your partnering teams to come to an agreed-on and shared prioritization plan. You're setting expectations in terms of value, impact, and timeline, so it's worth taking the time to get it right—and in writing.

It has to be a collaborative process. Disappearing into a dark room somewhere and emerging hours later with a carefully ordered list of how you'll prioritize your work will get you nowhere fast. Working through the concerns, needs, goals, and fixations of your partnering teams, on the other hand, will keep your work—and its impact on their success—top of mind.

Remember what they used to say in math class: *show your work*. Getting to the right answer is no victory at all if we don't get there together.

When priorities attack

When you need to choose between a variety of projects that are all clamoring for your attention and you simply don't have the bandwidth to do them all, it's time to take a different approach. Maybe for a while you've been able to use your prioritization simply as a method of ordering when you'll do each project and how much time you'll commit to each one. But at some point, you'll realize you can't do it all. That's when it's time to call in the cavalry and outsource some of your work to other people and tools.

Surface work can sometimes be handled by someone on the team who has attended your Surface workshop (see how that works?) or by some form of automation to smooth out the rough edges. If nobody on the team has taken your Surface workshop, you might book one for them now.

At HubSpot, we created an internal editor tool that applies the rules of our style guide and offers suggestions and corrections when it finds a mistake. Content creators simply paste their content into the tool, and the tool highlights the errors, offers hints and suggestions for revision, and links to the relevant part of the style guide for more detail.

This tool was based on an earlier, open-sourced version of something similar that's still available today, so building your own version might not be as much of a pipe dream as you think. It's fully worth the time required to create and maintain it, since it takes the most repetitive Surface corrections (spelling, punctuation, clichés, jargon, and so on) off your plate. Check out the Resources section for more ideas about building your own editor bot.

Surface work can also, in a pinch, be handled by a free tool like Grammarly or Hemingway. Are free tools ideal? Will they strictly follow your own style guide? Probably not. But asking people to use available tools before coming to you can free up an enormous amount of your time. Remember, since your time is best spent on the deeper layers of the stack, your job is to:

1. teach and empower other people in your organization to do more Surface work themselves, and
2. establish which tools they can use to check their Surface work without your help.

It takes a little time and effort to get the machinery in motion, but you'll soon be able to teach, delegate, and automate your way out of the morass of Surface work.

The hardest part of this process is actually letting the Surface work go. It is hard, in the moment, to say no to someone who asks you to give something a "quick look." But acquiescing not only keeps other people from learning and applying these skills and becoming more self-sufficient; it also reinforces in their minds that this is the only kind of work you do. Let it go.

Finding support

At some point, even the number of high-priority projects you're able to handle at the speed they need to be completed will become too much. Everyone will agree that your bandwidth has reached its limits. And *this* is where the conversation about headcount usually starts.

When the teams you're working with have had a direct hand in helping you build out your roadmap, yet there are still plenty of high-complexity, high-risk problems that need content support, that's usually when the teams themselves start advocating for headcount. The stakes are simply too high not to invest resources now. They'll move heaven and earth—and often, their very own headcount allocation—to get the content support they now know they need.

It's also possible you'll just have to work with what you have. Not all organizations will be able to hire new dedicated content people, no matter how much they'd like to. This may be due to economic hardship, the growth stage of your company, or a million other things that have nothing to do with how respected or valued you and your abilities are.

Whoever your organization is equipped to empower with content responsibilities can be your new team of content designers. Maybe it will be a cross-functional group that wants to run point for content needs on their team. Maybe it will be a blend that will evolve over time. The point is not to get too tied to a particular mechanism, job title, or organizational structure for improving the quality of content work overall. It's almost always more effective to take a pragmatic approach and work with what you've got.

Of course, by now, you're doing a lot to add more arrows to this particular quiver. By getting good content in front of people as often as you can, by running workshops that teach them how to help themselves as much as they can, you're building your organization's content capabilities by leaps and bounds. Not by fighting for headcount or by adding complexities to anyone's process—just by leading the way, showing your work, trusting the capabilities of others, and cultivating content champions wherever you can.

Even if you're the only content person in your organization, you can have an outsized impact by working with others who can share the load, and by focusing your efforts more and more on the deeper layers of the full content stack.

SUPPORTING A CONTENT PRACTICE

Regardless of job title, people all over your organization now care deeply about content because they've seen how it affects the work they do. How can you keep cultivating this newfound culture of content? How can you keep your new army of content folks interested, engaged, and sharp?

Whether you hire people from outside or just work with the people already on hand, you'll need the same systems to support them and keep them in tune. There are a number of ways to support the practice of content at your organization, no matter which or how many people are involved in the pursuit.

Content critiques

Give colleagues a chance to teach and learn from one another by setting up a regular time for them to share their in-progress content work, ask for feedback, and improve their skills in the context of a lovingly rendered content critique.

Peer-to-peer learning doesn't just improve the content under scrutiny; it also helps content creators think more deeply about their writing. Perspectives from other writers on other teams operating in other business contexts can lead to new approaches and results. And inviting people from all over the company to attend can widen the circle of colleagues who understand the scope of full-stack content design.

Most people will get heartburn at first when you suggest they put their rough drafts in front of their peers for feedback, so it's helpful to set some ground rules that will put people at ease. A good content critique follows much the same format as a good design review, so consider running yours along the same lines. Look in the Resources section for more help with running good critiques.

Content book club

Books clubs are perennially popular ways to get people engaged in a subject, talking about issues, and staying up to date with the latest thinking in the field. I've seen people get scared off by the level of commitment involved in a traditional book club, however, so you might consider framing this as more of a reading club that shares and discusses briefs, articles, talks, blog posts, or books.

But don't just set up a Slack channel to share links; without accountability of some sort, few will take the time to read most of what's shared, so make sure you plan regular opportunities to discuss as a group. You can set up recurring reminders to help people remember what you'll be discussing next, and who will be responsible for leading the conversation. It's often a good idea to rotate responsibility for facilitating the discussion so no one person is always on—or off—the hook every time.

Content networking

Set up time to chat with content people at other companies you admire. This can be a mutual "ask me anything" session where you talk about things you've learned or are still struggling with. How do they approach project prioritization? How do they do content work across the full stack? What has worked for them as they've scaled and grown their content practice over time? What hasn't worked out so well?

Not sure where to find such lovely people to chat with? You can start with the people you talk about in your book club. Authors, podcast hosts and their guests, people doing interesting work mentioned in books and articles, conference speakers you've seen in person or on YouTube, people you've connected with (or would like to connect with) on LinkedIn—the list goes on. If you don't feel you have the network required for this sort of thing, that's kind of the point. Forcing yourself to reach out to people in the industry you'd like to learn from is how they all started, too.

Thirty-day writing sprints

For the people who ask you how to get better at writing, the answer is: practice. Challenge these folks to a thirty-day sprint of writing for fifteen minutes every day, with the goal of getting to what the writer Anne Lamott calls a "shitty first draft."

You can set up an informal sprint group and support each other with daily prompts. This will keep folks from trying to get too fancy (developing fully fleshed-out blog posts, or writing the Great American Novel, for instance) when the goal is to get comfortable with the practice of dumping words out of your brain. Tell them they can worry about the editing and shaping of it later.

The stripped-down version of this writing sprint practice is really:

1. write like crap
2. every day
3. about not much at all

And it actually works. In fact, it's the *only* way to get better at writing, as we writers know. If you can recruit content creators when they're on fire with enthusiasm for writing and content—and many will be after attending one of your fabulous workshops—they'll have a real shot at developing their writing skills in this way. Even if they only stick to it for a couple of weeks, they'll learn very quickly how to keep typing through thick and thin.

THE BIG PICTURE

Imagine no longer seeing your job as a series of battles to be fought, no more us against them, no more peering over your reading glasses at the philistines who just don't get how you feel about exclamation marks, and never will. A healthy, full-stack content ecosystem creates a culture in which not just content professionals, but *everyone* who touches content, can truly grow, expand their impact, and thrive.

Once you commit to establishing a full-stack content practice in your organization, once you shift your focus to educating and empowering all the non-writers in your company to step into their power as content superheroes, that's when it happens. That's when the mindset shift starts to take hold. And that's when people start asking you to contribute in the very ways you've been hoping to.

CONCLUSION

SO MUCH OF THIS BOOK has been about the subtle art of letting go. And there's a good reason for that.

We agreed at the start of this conversation that we, as content people, need to get over ourselves and our need to *own all the words*. It's just not helping, that attitude. It doesn't get us a seat at the table. It doesn't demonstrate our value. It doesn't really achieve much of anything except an inner sense of smugness and victimhood.

So let's just stop. Let's replace that attitude with one that conveys our enthusiasm, empowers our colleagues, and lightens our loads.

The point isn't to teach and train and automate our way out of a job. The point is to encourage absolutely everybody in our organizations to own some part of the job of content design, so they all:

1. have a clearer idea of what the full stack of content design truly entails and can do for their goals,
2. know where and how they can contribute to great content themselves, and
3. recognize when it's time to call in a specialist—a content pro like you and the folks on your (soon-to-be-growing) team.

Steps one and two will help you clear the decks so you can pick and choose where you spend your quality time. Step three will make it clear if and when you need to add strength to your team.

None of this has a dang thing to do with where we all stand on the use of an Oxford comma, I'm afraid. But it does have to do with giving you your life and sanity back. It will also give you the chance to see light bulbs come on in the minds of your colleagues, illuminating your shared problem spaces with crisp, clear, compelling content that *everyone* has had a hand in creating.

Once you've achieved all that wonderfulness, it's time to kick back and enjoy the fruits of success. Wait, no, that's not right either. Because this is when the real work truly begins.

Nobody is better situated to keep a beady eye on what it is we're persuading others to believe—about ourselves, our products, and the way the world works—than content folks are. Content can convince people the world is a terrifying place that's relentlessly spiraling downward. Or it can say there's some good in this world, Frodo, and it's worth fighting for.

Everything you do—as a professional, as a team leader, as an encourager, as an aspiring strategic seat holder—tells the world who you are and what you stand for. Seeking out and supporting the hidden writer in everyone sends a message that we're all in this together. That together we win.

It's a pretty big deal to finally get that seat at the table you've been clamoring for. It's an even bigger deal when you manage to build your own table and invite everyone to join you in creating something new. Now that you have a growing and carefully cultivated content practice in your organization, what are you going to do with it?

ACKNOWLEDGMENTS

THANKS TO EVERYONE WHO told me that writing this book was a terrific idea, starting with Kristina Halvorson, who said it first. Thanks also to Dan Tyre, Richard Waystack, Hannah Fleishman, Danielle Kowalski, Scott Kubie, and Jami Oetting, who either encouraged me at the outset or egged me on every step of the way. Sarah Winters and Aaron Burgess both reviewed an early manuscript of this book and gave me valuable feedback and love, for which I am grateful beyond words. Ann Handley took me out for dinner and reassured me that I wasn't alone in my lifelong love for newsletters and what they can do.

Thanks to Christopher O'Donnell, Josh Porter, Tim Merrill, and Libby Maurer, who supported and sponsored the growth of content design at HubSpot before many product people even knew what it was. Thanks to Brian Halligan, who didn't blink when I cornered him in a hallway in 2010 and told him HubSpot needed an internal newsletter, said that sounded fantastic, and let me take it from there. Thanks to everyone at HubSpot who has loved, read, and submitted to the WIN. Writing this newsletter and serving as an amplifier for the unique personality and verve of this remarkable company has always been the best part of my job. Thank you for letting me hold up a mirror to you every week and remind you what excellent people you are.

RESOURCES

There are a handful of books and links I recommend to people whenever they ask me where to get started with content design. This isn't by any means an exhaustive list, but it's a good place to begin.

- Sarah Winters wrote the book *Content Design* (under the name Sarah Richards) and gave us all a focus and framework for what content design was and should be. Her emphasis on first doing content discovery and research, then centering the design on what the user actually needs (and not what the designer or organization wishes to say) was revolutionary when it came out and continues to be a definitive guide. This book also contains some very helpful recommendations for how to run effective content critiques, do pair writing, conduct user research, and develop several other practical skills.
- See also her team's *Readability Guidelines*, which will help anyone who wants to make their style guide less focused on old-fashioned and frequently irrelevant rules of grammar and punctuation and more focused on how to create truly useful, accessible, inclusive content (http://bkaprt.com/ccd12/05-01/). Better yet, it's all based on evidence and research, rather than personal preference for this rule or that.
- We've been treated to a wave of sterling books recently on the nuts and bolts of UX writing. One that stands out is *Writing Is Designing: Words and the User Experience* by Andy Welfle and Michael Metts, both for its thoroughness and use of real-life examples, and for how it incorporates the voices of real people doing this work in a variety of industries and fields. Read this book to learn more about how to do great UX writing, and to get introduced to some of the smartest, kindest people working on it today.

- Rachel McConnell's book *Why You Need a Content Team and How to Build One* is a terrific resource for content people on teams of all sizes and stages of growth, from the solo practitioner to a large, globally integrated team. She helps you diagnose which stage you're in and what you might need to advance to the next level. It's an invaluable guide, especially if you're building a content team for the first time.
- Ann Handley's book *Everybody Writes: Your Go-To Guide to Creating Ridiculously Good Content* is what I give people who tell me they want to get better at writing but don't know where to start. It's empowering, practical, and down-to-earth. Ann's newsletter for writers, *Total Annarchy,* is a fortnightly infusion of insights, ideas, encouragement, and fun. Shenanigans, as Ann would say. It's one newsletter you will read, learn from, and laugh at, every time (http://bkaprt.com/ccd12/05-02/).
- Donna Lichaw's book *The User's Journey: Storymapping Products That People Love* will not just remind you how much you love the movie *Back to the Future*; it will also give you a clear, actionable model for how to apply the principles of storytelling to create truly user-centered experiences. A lot of people like to *say* the user is the hero, but then create content that's clearly centered on what the company wants the user to do. This book will snap you out of that trap. It's also a great book to give to people you work with, so you have a shared language and vision for what you're trying to do.
- Shopify built Rory, an editor bot that applies the rules of their style guide to their help documentation (http://bkaprt.com/ccd12/05-03/). It was adapted from an earlier, open-source editor tool called Alex (http://bkaprt.com/ccd12/05-04/). The source code for both Rory and Alex is available for anyone to use and adapt (although even open-source tools have license requirements, so make sure you comply with those). Alex comes complete with standard rulesets (for inclusive language, clichés, jargon, and more) that will likely apply to your style guide. Add a few rulesets specific to your house style, set it up on your server, and you're good to go.

- The Content + UX Slack group is a must for anyone interested in chatting about content design, learning more about UX writing, or meeting helpful, smart people who do great things with words. Ask questions, find a job, explore new topics, and make new friends from all over the world (http://bkaprt.com/ccd12/05-05/).

Content design is increasingly becoming a very large and boisterous party, one to which I'm delighted to report that newcomers and fresh perspectives are most heartily welcome. You'll find an open door to the party through any of these resources, but then you will quickly find yourself drawn into some fascinating side conversations and brilliant new friends to go deeper with. Please join us, and then tell us what you've learned.

REFERENCES

Shortened URLs are numbered sequentially; the related long URLs are listed below for reference.

Chapter 1

01-01 http://www.jjg.net/elements/pdf/elements.pdf

Resources

05-01 https://readabilityguidelines.co.uk

05-02 https://annhandley.com/newsletter/

05-03 https://ux.shopify.com/rorybot-automated-content-style-checking-4d42946ae318

05-04 http://alexjs.com

05-05 https://contentandux.org

INDEX

ABOUT THE AUTHOR

Beth Dunn is a content and communications leader, speaker, author, and coach. She pioneered the content design practice at HubSpot, then developed and led the global HubSpot content design team. Her workshops, classes, exercises, and guides have helped scores of leaders, practitioners, and teams design better content, confidently and at scale. Beth Dunn lives on Cape Cod in her tiny hometown with a charming husband and some quality cats.

Printed in the USA
CPSIA information can be obtained
at www.ICGtesting.com
JSHW041356030923
47344JS00001B/2

9 781087 952512